HOW TO USE YOUR DICTIONARY

LEARNING SKILLS SERIES

HOW TO USE YOUR DICTIONARY

Roger Lewis and Martin Pugmire

Published by
CollinsEducational Ltd
77-85 Fulham Palace Road
Hammersmith
London W6 8JB

First published in 1993

The National Extension College (NEC) is an educational trust with a distinguished body of trustees. Since it was established in 1963, it has pioneered the development of flexible learning for adults. NEC is actively developing innovative materials and systems for distance learning on over 100 courses, from basic skills to degree and professional training. Working in partnership with CollinsEducational, NEC can now offer the best in flexible learning materials to the widest possible audience and further its aim of extending educational opportunities for all.

About the authors:

Roger Lewis has taught in primary and secondary schools, adult and higher education. He is currently the BP Professor of Learning Development at the University of Humberside. He has written many books for students and teachers. Roger has gained most of his own qualifications through independent study.

Martin Pugmire is a teacher of English language and literature, and also helps to train teachers. He previously taught at a technical college and lectured at the North East Wales Institute of Higher Education. He has also worked part-time for the Open University and has published on teaching literature through television.

The publishers wish to thank Tim Burton for his invaluable editorial expertise.

British Library Cataloguing-in-Publication Data
A catalogue record for
this book is
available from the
British Library.

ISBN 0 00 322348 5

Typeset by Squires Graphics. Cover design by Information Design Workshop. Printed in Great Britain at the University Press, Cambridge

Contents

UNIT 1 INTRODUCTION

What is this book about?

We have written this for anyone who is concerned with words, and who wants to use them more exactly. The dictionary is our most valuable single resource when we are trying to write or speak more fluently, and it is important that we should use it to the full. Tutors often say 'Use your dictionary', but don't always help students to do this.

So we hope:

- to help you to make the fullest use of your dictionary, and to show you how valuable it can be;
- through doing this, to help you to improve your powers of expression – in speaking and in writing.

How do I use this book?

You may be studying in one of the following ways:

- You may have bought the book from a bookshop and plan to work through it on your own.
- You may be a student who has been advised by a tutor or teacher to look at certain parts of this book.

You can use the book flexibly. You may want to work through it unit by unit, and you might be surprised at how many uses the dictionary has. Alternatively you may only be interested in one or two particular aspects of dictionary use. If this is the case you can turn to these parts of the book.

How is the book organised?

It is important to understand how the book has been put together, so you can use it to the full. This is not a textbook; it is a book designed to help you to learn for yourself. So we have included a number of special features.

Self-Assessment Questions (SAQs)

SAQs are always indicated by this symbol. When you see this symbol, stop, read over the question and write down your own answer. Only when you have answered the question for yourself should you go on to see how we have answered it.

Some SAQs will have 'right' answers. But most are matters of emphasis and various answers are possible, so you should not worry if you disagree slightly with us. Please remember this; don't expect your answers to be exactly the same as ours.

We recommend that you use a sheet of A4 paper or card to cover the text beneath an SAQ to stop yourself reading the answer before you have written down your own.

The SAQs in this book take the place of a teacher. They aim to:

- get you involved in what you are reading;
- give you practice in using a dictionary;
- allow you to keep an eye on your own progress through the book.

What this unit is about

Each of the subsequent units in this book begins with this heading. In 'What this unit is about' you'll find an outline of what the unit contains.

Pre-test and Post-test

We have included a 'pre-test' which you can use, if you wish, to decide which parts of the book to study. The steps are:

- to try to answer all the pre-test questions (honestly, of course!);
- to try to realise that, if you are unable to answer yes to the questions under any unit heading, you need to study that unit.

At the end of the book we have also included a 'post-test'. You can choose whether to answer the questions in the 'post-test' after each unit, or to leave them all until the end of the book

How long will it take?

If you are dipping into the book, then clearly it takes as long as you choose to spend on it. If you are working through it systematically, then it will take about three or four months. But students vary greatly in how long they spend.

You may feel that you have to spend quite a long time working on some of the SAQs in this book. But your time will be well spent. Be patient and bear in mind that:

- while you are learning to use your dictionary you are also learning to use language more effectively.

What do I need to work through this book?

To study this book you will need:

- this book;
- paper and pen;
- a dictionary.

We have also provided five blank pages for your notes at the end of this book.

You can use any general dictionary. If, however, you wish to buy a dictionary specially to use with this book we recommend the *Collins New Compact English Dictionary* (ask for the most up-to-date edition). This is the dictionary most frequently referred to for examples.

Pre-test

Answer 'yes' or 'no' to all the following questions.

Unit 2

1 Open your dictionary. Can you list five different kinds of information it provides about words?

2 Has your dictionary been designed:

- as a general help, easily carried around with you? Yes/No
- as a comprehensive guide (i.e. not easily carried and very detailed)? Yes/No

Can you give your reasons for your answers?

(If you answer *no* to either of these questions, study Unit 2.)

Unit 3

1 Can you state reasons why the information given in a dictionary is laid out as it is?

2 Given an entry in a dictionary, can you find straightaway:

- whether the given word is a noun, adjective, verb or other part of speech? Yes/No
- which other words are related to the word, or can be formed from it? Yes/No

3 Do you understand what the following signs and abbreviations mean? Write your answers in the spaces provided.

- n. [ ]
- v. [ ]
- [orig. unkn.] [ ]
- colloq. [ ]
- a. [ ]
- adv. [ ]

(If you answer *no* to any of these questions, study Unit 3.)

Unit 4

1 When meeting an unusual or difficult word can you use your dictionary to help you understand it:

- quickly? Yes/No
- every time? Yes/No

2 Can you use your dictionary to find synonyms? Yes/No

3 Can you state at least three reasons why the dictionary can never give any more than guidance to a particular word's meaning?

(If you answer *no* to any of these questions, study Unit 4.)

Unit 5

1 Do you ever worry about your spelling? Yes/No

2 Do you feel the need to adopt a 'spelling strategy'? Yes/No

3 Do you have difficulty in finding a word you cannot spell in the dictionary? Yes/No

4 Do you ever end up with the wrong spelling even when you have checked a word in your dictionary? Yes/No

5 Do you have spelling problems when you need to modify a word because of the way in which you are using it (e.g. to turn 'buy' into 'bought')? Yes/No

(If you answer *yes* to any of these questions, study Unit 5.)

Unit 6

1 Can you understand what your dictionary tells you about pronunciation? Yes/No

2 Can you say why the dictionary can never be a final authority on matters of pronunciation?

(If you answer *no* to either of these questions, study Unit 6.)

Unit 7

1 Can you find, and do you understand, what your dictionary tells you about the history of a word? Yes/No

2 Do you know the limitations of your dictionary in helping you to deal with problems which arise from the changes in the meaning of a word in the course of time? Yes/No

3 Do you know what to do when your dictionary lets you down? Yes/No

(If you answer *no* to any of these questions, study Unit 7.)

UNIT 2 WHAT IS A DICTIONARY?

What this unit is about

By the time you have finished your work on this unit, you should be able to:

- list the five distinct sorts of information that you will find in a good general dictionary;
- decide what size of general dictionary is best suited to your daily needs;
- explain what larger general dictionaries are designed for, and when you may find them useful.

Introduction

What do you really expect to find when you open a book with the word 'dictionary' written on the cover? Think about this for a moment, and note down your answer.

Use your A4 sheet to cover up our response.

You probably expect an alphabetical list of most of the words in the language, with entries to tell you about each word in turn.

It is quite easy to separate the three ideas involved in this description.

They are:

- that a dictionary is alphabetical;
- that a dictionary tries to include as many of the words of our language as it can;
- that a dictionary tells you about each word.

The first of these is simple.

The second is rather more complicated, when you think about it. Small dictionaries cannot list as many words as big ones do, and there are some dictionaries that only deal with the words of a special subject. A dictionary of place-names is an obvious example. These points will come up again later in this unit.

The third is quite vague. We need to work out what kinds of things 'a dictionary tells you about each word'.

To do this, study the extract in *Figure 1* below. It is a reproduction of the first page of a dictionary.

2 In the space provided on the next page list three of the different sorts of information that this dictionary is giving you about words. Don't spend longer than five minutes on this, and don't worry about using the correct terms. Remember to use your A4 sheet.

A

A[1] /eɪ/ *n.* (also **a**) (*pl.* **As** or **A's**) **1** the first letter of the alphabet. **2** *Mus.* the sixth note of the diatonic scale of C major. **3** the first hypothetical person or example. **4** the highest class or category (of roads, academic marks, etc.). **5** (usu. **a**) *Algebra* the first known quantity. **6** a human blood type of the ABO system. □ **A1** /eɪ 'wʌn/ **1** *Naut.* **a** a first-class vessel in Lloyd's Register of Shipping. **b** first-class. **2** *colloq.* excellent, first-rate. **A1**, **A2**, etc. the standard paper sizes, each half the previous one, e.g. A4 = 297 × 210 mm, A5 = 210 × 148 mm. **from A to B** from one place to another (*a means of getting from A to B*). **from A to Z** over the entire range, completely.

A[2] /eɪ/ *abbr.* (also **A.**) **1** *Brit.* (of films) classified as suitable for an adult audience but not necessarily for children. ¶ Now replaced by *PG*. **2** = A LEVEL. **3** ampere(s). **4** answer. **5** Associate of. **6** atomic (energy etc.).

a[1] /ə, eɪ/ *adj.* (also **an** before a vowel) (called the indefinite article) **1** (as an unemphatic substitute) one, some, any. **2** one like (*a Judas*). **3** one single (*not a thing in sight*). **4** the same (*all of a size*). **5** in, to, or for each (*twice a year*; *£20 a man*; *seven a side*). [weakening of OE *ān* one; sense 5 orig. = A[2]]

a[2] /ə/ *prep.* (usu. as *prefix*) **1** to, towards (*ashore*; *aside*). **2** (with verb in pres. part. or infin.) in the process of; in a specified state (*a-hunting*; *a-wandering*; *abuzz*; *aflutter*). **3** on (*afire*; *afoot*). **4** in (*nowadays*). [weakening of OE prep. *an*, *on* (see ON)]

a[3] *abbr.* atto-.

Å *abbr.* ångström(s).

a-[1] /eɪ, æ/ *prefix* not, without (*amoral*; *agnostic*; *apetalous*). [Gk *a-*, or L f. Gk, or F f. L f. Gk]

a-[2] /ə/ *prefix* implying motion onward or away, adding intensity to verbs of motion (*arise*; *awake*). [OE *a-*, orig. *ar-*]

a-[3] /ə/ *prefix* to, at, or into a state (*adroit*; *agree*; *amass*; *avenge*). [ME *a-* (= OF prefix *a-*), (f. F) f. L *ad-* to, at]

a-[4] /ə/ *prefix* **1** from, away (*abridge*). **2** of (*akin*; *anew*). **3** out, utterly (*abash*; *affray*). **4** in, on, engaged in, etc. (see A[2]). [sense 1 f. ME *a-*, OF *a-*, f. L *ab*; sense 2 f. ME *a-* f. OE *of* prep.; sense 3 f. ME, AF *a-* = OF *e-*, *es-* f. L *ex*]

a-[5] /ə, æ/ *prefix* assim. form of AD- before *sc*, *sp*, *st*.

-a[1] /ə/ *suffix* forming nouns from Greek, Latin, and Romanic feminine singular, esp.: **1** ancient or Latinized modern names of animals and plants (*amoeba*; *campanula*). **2** oxides (*alumina*). **3** geographical names (*Africa*). **4** ancient or Latinized modern feminine names (*Lydia*; *Hilda*).

-a[2] /ə/ *suffix* forming plural nouns from Greek and Latin neuter plural, esp. names (often from modern Latin) of zoological groups (*phenomena*; *Carnivora*).

-a[3] /ə/ *suffix colloq. sl.* **1** of (*kinda*; *coupla*). **2** have (*mighta*; *coulda*). **3** to (*oughta*).

AA *abbr.* **1** Automobile Association. **2** Alcoholics Anonymous. **3** *Mil.* anti-aircraft. **4** *Brit.* (of films) classified as suitable for persons of over 14 years. ¶ Now replaced by *PG*.

AAA *abbr.* **1** (in the UK) Amateur Athletic Association. **2** American Automobile Association. **3** Australian Automobile Association.

A. & M. *abbr.* (Hymns) Ancient and Modern.

A. & R. *abbr.* **1** artists and recording. **2** artists and repertoire.

aardvark /'ɑːdvɑːk/ *n.* a nocturnal mammal of southern Africa, *Orycteropus afer*, with a tubular snout and a long extendible tongue, that feeds on termites. Also called *ant-bear*, *earth-hog*. [Afrik. f. *aarde* earth + *vark* pig]

aardwolf /'ɑːdwʊlf/ *n.* (*pl.* **aardwolves** /-wʊlvz/) an African mammal, *Proteles cristatus*, of the hyena family, with grey fur and black stripes, that feeds on insects. [Afrik. f. *aarde* earth + *wolf* wolf]

Aaron's beard /'eərənz/ *n.* any of several plants, esp. rose of Sharon (*Hypericum calycinum*). [ref. to Ps. 133:2]

Aaron's rod /'eərənz/ *n.* any of several tall plants, esp. the great mullein (*Verbascum thapsus*). [ref. to Num. 17:8]

A'asia *abbr.* Australasia.

aasvogel /'ɑːs,fəʊg(ə)l/ *n.* a vulture. [Afrik. f. *aas* carrion + *vogel* bird]

AAU *abbr.* *US* Amateur Athletic Union.

AB[1] /eɪ'biː/ *n.* a human blood type of the ABO system.

AB[2] *abbr.* **1** able rating or seaman. **2** *US* Bachelor of Arts. [sense 1 f. *able-bodied*; sense 2 f. L *Artium Baccalaureus*]

ab- /əb, æb/ *prefix* off, away, from (*abduct*; *abnormal*; *abuse*). [F or L]

aba /'æbə/ *n.* (also **abba**, **abaya** /ə'beɪjə/) a sleeveless outer garment worn by Arabs. [Arab. *'abā'*]

abaca /'æbəkə/ *n.* **1** Manila hemp. **2** the plant, *Musa textilis*, yielding this. [Sp. *abacá*]

aback /ə'bæk/ *adv.* **1** *archaic* backwards, behind. **2** *Naut.* (of a sail) pressed against the mast by a head wind. □ **take aback 1** surprise, disconcert (*your request took me aback*; *I was greatly taken aback by the news*). **2** (as **taken aback**) (of a ship) with the sails pressed against the mast by a head wind. [OE *on bæc* (as A[2], BACK)]

abacus /'æbəkəs/ *n.* (*pl.* **abacuses**) **1** an oblong frame with rows of wires or grooves along which beads are slid, used for calculating. **2** *Archit.* the flat slab on top of a capital, supporting the architrave. [L f. Gk *abax abakos* slab, drawing-board, f. Heb. *'āḇāq* dust]

Abaddon /ə'bæd(ə)n/ *n.* **1** hell. **2** the Devil (Rev. 9: 11). [Heb., = destruction]

abaft /ə'bɑːft/ *adv.* & *prep.* *Naut.* —*adv.* in the stern half of a ship. —*prep.* nearer the stern than; aft of. [A[2] + *-baft* f. OE *beæftan* f. *be* BY + *æftan* behind]

abalone /,æbə'ləʊnɪ/ *n.* any mollusc of the genus *Haliotis*, with a shallow ear-shaped shell having respiratory holes, and lined with mother-of-pearl, e.g. the ormer. [Amer. Sp. *abulón*]

abandon /ə'bænd(ə)n/ *v.* & *n.* —*v.tr.* **1** give up completely or before completion (*abandoned hope*; *abandoned the game*). **2 a** forsake or desert (a person or a post of responsibility). **b** leave or desert (a motor vehicle or ship). **3 a** give up to another's control or mercy. **b** *refl.* yield oneself completely to a passion or impulse. —*n.* lack of inhibition or restraint; reckless freedom of manner. □□ **abandoner** *n.* **abandonment** *n.* [ME f. OF *abandoner* f. *à bandon* under control ult. f. LL *bannus*, *-um* BAN]

abandoned /ə'bænd(ə)nd/ *adj.* **1 a** (of a person) deserted, forsaken (*an abandoned child*). **b** (of a building, vehicle, etc.) left empty or unused (*an abandoned cottage*; *an abandoned ship*). **2** (of a person or behaviour) unrestrained, profligate.

abase /ə'beɪs/ *v.tr.* & *refl.* humiliate or degrade (another person or oneself). □□ **abasement** *n.* [ME f. OF *abaissier* (as A-[3], *baissier* to lower ult. f. LL *bassus* short of stature): infl. by BASE[2]]

abash /ə'bæʃ/ *v.tr.* (usu. as **abashed** *adj.*) embarrass, disconcert. □□ **abashment** *n.* [ME f. OF *esbaïr* (*es-* = A-[4] 3, *baïr* astound or *baer* yawn)]

abate /ə'beɪt/ *v.* **1** *tr.* & *intr.* make or become less

Figure 1 Page 1, *Concise Oxford Dictionary.* (Oxford University Press) 8th Edition, 1990

(continued opposite)

You may have listed any three of the following, perhaps by different names. You may even have split some of them into two items:

- meaning (including examples of use); e.g. 'abaft' means 'in the stern half of a ship'; the example given in italics after 'from A to B';
- spelling;
- grammar (parts of speech); e.g. 'aba' is a noun (n.);
- history of a word; e.g. the Old English (OE) origin of 'aback';
- pronunciation; e.g. after the 'Aaron's beard' entry, /ˈeərənz/.

Now look again at the extract. Can you find further examples of my five kinds of information? You will find some of them hard to recognise at this stage, but the next unit will deal with this. These five sorts of information about words are what a good general dictionary will give you.

Different kinds of dictionary

Not all dictionaries are 'general', of course. The easiest way to explain why is to look again at the extract in *Figure 1*. It has a number of faults.

3

List any faults that strike you.

Why are these faults in the dictionary? Decide on the reason for yourself, and write it down below.

My list is as follows:

- The extract is hard to understand fully, since it uses a lot of abbreviations.
- The print is small.
- Really obscure words are missed out (e.g. 'abacist', the word for a person who uses an abacus).
- It would be a great help to be given more examples of how people use the words that are listed.

The reason for these faults is surely lack of space. The shortcomings are a result of trying to make a one-volume dictionary.

It would be quite easy to avoid all these faults. You could design a dictionary that would use fewer abbreviations and larger print, include all the words in English, and offer many examples of use. You would end up with something like the *Oxford English Dictionary*. Unfortunately, this runs to 16 volumes and (in 1993) costs well over £1000.

This highlights the problem of the general dictionary. If it really does its job well, a general dictionary is extremely large and expensive. If, on the other hand, it is short and cheap, it is likely to show the kinds of faults that I have just been pointing out.

One way to avoid some of these faults is to create a specialist dictionary. There are two distinct ways of doing this. A dictionary can specialise in one sort of information about words. This leaves lots of space for detail even in a small book, and a rather larger one can give you a tremendous amount of specialist information about a very large number of words. A dictionary of pronunciation is an example of this sort of specialist dictionary. Other common examples are etymological dictionaries (specialising in the history of words), and dictionaries that specialise in translations.

The other approach is to select the words to be included according to a special subject. Thus a dictionary of place names only lists place names, to state the obvious. This at once frees a great deal of space for information about the words that *are* listed.

This kind of specialist dictionary may include words that a general dictionary would miss out, such as highly specialist terms and even proper names. Thus a dictionary of linguistic terms will list words like 'morph' and 'phoneme', and may include entries under the names of people important in the science of linguistics. Indeed, if the special subject of a dictionary was names, as in a dictionary of surnames or of place names, *none* of the words listed would appear in a general dictionary, except of course for names like 'Smith' or 'Turner' which might appear in their other usage.

The importance of all this is that different dictionaries are good at different jobs. To make this point clear, study *Figure 2 Extracts A, B, C* and *D* which illustrate more first pages of dictionaries. Then answer SAQs 4 and 5 on page 20.

A

AALTO, Alvar (1898–1976) an important modern architect, and certainly pre-eminent in his native Finland. Started neo-classically, in a typically Scandinavian idiom, *c.* 1923–5, and turned to the INTERNATIONAL MODERN with his excellent Library at Viipuri (1927–35), Convalescent Home at Paimio (1929–33), and factory with workers' housing at Sumila (1936–9, with large additions of 1951–7). He possessed a strong feeling for materials and their characters, which, Finland being a country of forests, inspired him to use timber widely. He also invented bent plywood furniture (1932). Timber figured prominently in his Finnish Pavilion at the Paris Exhibition of 1937 and in the Villa Mairea at Noormarkku (1938). Aalto's most original works date from after the Second World War. By then he had evolved a language entirely his own, quite unconcerned with current clichés, yet in its vigorous display of curved walls and single-pitched roofs, in its play with brick and timber, entirely in harmony with the international trend towards plastically more expressive *ensembles*. The principal works are a Hall of Residence at the Massachusetts Institute of Technology, Cambridge, Mass. (1947–9), with a curved front and staircases projecting out of the wall and climbing up diagonally; the Village Hall at Säynatsälo (1951); the Pensions Institute at Helsinki (1952–7), a more straightforward job; the church at Imatra (1952–8), on a completely free plan; and the Hall of Culture at Helsinki (1958).

ABACUS. The flat slab on the top of a CAPITAL: in Greek Doric a thick square slab; in Greek Ionic, Tuscan, Roman Doric and Ionic, square with the lower edge moulded; in Corinthian and Composite with concave sides and the corners cut off. *See figure 64.*

ABADIE, Paul, *see* VAUDREMER.

ABBEY, *see* MONASTERY.

ABUTMENT. Solid masonry placed to counteract the lateral thrust of a VAULT or ARCH. *See figure 4.*

ACANTHUS. A plant with thick, fleshy, scalloped leaves used on carved ornament of Corinthian and Composite CAPITALS and on other mouldings. *See figure 1.*

Fig. 1. Acanthus.

ACROPOLIS. The citadel of a Greek city, built at its highest point and containing the chief temples and public buildings, as at Athens.

ACROTERIA. Plinths for statues or ornaments placed at the apex and ends of a PEDIMENT; also, more loosely, both the plinths and what stands on them. *See figure 2.*

ADAM, Robert (1728–92), the greatest British architect of the later C18, was equally if not more brilliant as a decorator, furniture designer, etc., for which his name is still a household word. He is comparable in his chaste and rather epicene elegance with his French contemporary SOUFFLOT, but without Soufflot's chilly solemnity. He was a typically hard-headed Scot, canny and remorselessly ambitious, yet with a tender, romantic side to his character as well. Both facets were reflected in his work, which

7

Figure 2 Extract A: Penguin Dictionary of Architecture.

A

A (*the letter*), **-'s** eɪ, -z
a (*indefinite article*) eɪ (*strong form*), ə (*weak form*)
aardvark, -s 'ɑ:dvɑ:k, -s
Aaron, -s 'eərən, -z
aback ə'bæk
Abaco (*in Bahamas*) 'æbəkəʊ
abacus, -es 'æbəkəs, -ɪz
Abadan (*in Iran*) ˌæbə'dɑ:n [-'dæn]
Abaddon ə'bædən
abaft ə'bɑ:ft
abandon (*s.*) ə'bændən (abɑ̃dɔ̃)
abandon (*v.*), **-s, -ing, -ed/ly, -ment** ə'bændən, -z, -ɪŋ, -d/lɪ, -mənt
abas|e, -es, -ing, -ed, -ement ə'beɪs, -ɪz, -ɪŋ, -t, -mənt
abash, -es, -ing, -ed ə'bæʃ, -ɪz, -ɪŋ, -t
abatab|le, -ly ə'beɪtəb|l, -lɪ
abat|e, -es, -ing, -ed, -ement/s ə'beɪt, -s, -ɪŋ, -ɪd, -mənt/s
abatis (*sing.*) 'æbətɪs [-ti:]
abatis (*plur.*) 'æbəti:z
abatises (*plur.*) 'æbətɪsɪz
abattis, -es ə'bætɪs, -ɪz
abattoir, -s 'æbətwɑ:* [-twɔ:*], -z
Abba 'æbə
abbac|y, -ies 'æbəs|ɪ, -ɪz
Abbas 'æbəs [-bæs]
abbé, -s 'æbeɪ (abe), -z
abbess, -es 'æbes [-bɪs], -ɪz
Abbeville (*in France*) 'æbvi:l (abvil), (*in U.S.A.*) 'æbɪvɪl
abbey (**A.**), **-s** 'æbɪ, -z
abbot (**A.**), 'æbət, -s
Abbotsford 'æbətsfəd
abbotship, -s 'æbət-ʃɪp, -s
Abbott 'æbət
abbreviat|e, -es, -ing, -ed, -or/s ə'bri:vɪeɪt [vjeɪt], -s, -ɪŋ, -ɪd, -ə*/z
abbreviation, -s əˌbri:vɪ'eɪʃn, -z
abbreviatory ə'bri:vjətərɪ [-vɪət-, -vɪeɪt-]
abc, -'s ˌeɪbi:'si:, -z
Abdera æb'dɪərə
abdicant, -s 'æbdɪkənt, -s
abdicat|e, -es, -ing, -ed 'æbdɪkeɪt, -s, -ɪŋ, -ɪd
abdication, -s ˌæbdɪ'keɪʃn, -z
Abdiel 'æbdɪəl [-djəl]
abdomen, -s 'æbdəmen [æb'dəʊmen, -mɪn, -mən], -z
abdomin|al, -ally æb'dɒmɪn|l [əb-], -əlɪ
abduct, -s, -ing, -ed, -or/s æb'dʌkt [əb-], -s, -ɪŋ, -ɪd, -ə*/z
abduction, -s æb'dʌkʃn [əb-], -z
Abdulla, -s æb'dʌlə [əb-], -z
Abdy 'æbdɪ
Abe eɪb
abeam ə'bi:m
abecedarian ˌeɪbi:si:'deərɪən
A Becket ə'bekɪt
abed ə'bed
Abednego ˌæbed'ni:gəʊ [ə'bednɪgəʊ]
Abel (*biblical name, English name*) 'eɪbəl, (*foreign name*) 'ɑ:bəl
Abelard 'æbɪlɑ:d ['æbə-]
Abell 'eɪbəl
Abelmeholah ˌeɪbəlmɪ'həʊlə [-mə'h-]
Aberavon ˌæbə'rævən [-bɜ:'r-] (*Welsh* aber'avon)
Aberbrothock ˌæbə'brɒθək [-bɜ:'b-]
Note.—This place-name has to be pronounced ˌæbəbrə'θɒk [-bɜ:b-] *in Southey's 'Inchcape Rock'.*
Abercorn 'æbəkɔ:n
Abercrombie [**-by**] 'æbəkrʌmbɪ [-krɒm-, ˌ--'--]
Aberdare ˌæbə'deə* (*Welsh* aber'da:r)
Aberdeen, -shire ˌæbə'di:n, -ʃə* [-ˌʃɪə*]
aberdevine, -s ˌæbədə'vaɪn, -z
Aberdonian, -s ˌæbə'dəʊnjən [-nɪən], -z
Aberdour ˌæbə'daʊə*
Aberdovey ˌæbə'dʌvɪ (*Welsh* aber'dəvi)
Abergavenny (*family name*) ˌæbə'genɪ, (*place*) ˌæbəgə'venɪ (*Welsh* aberga'veni)
Abergele ˌæbə'gelɪ (*Welsh* aber'gele)
Abernethy ˌæbə'neθɪ [*in the S. also* -'ni:θɪ]
aberran|ce, -cy, -t æ'berən|s [ə'b-], -sɪ, -t
aberrat|e, -es, -ing, -ed 'æbəreɪt [-ber-], -s, -ɪŋ, -ɪd
aberration, -s ˌæbə'reɪʃn [-be'r-], -z
Abersychan ˌæbə'sɪkən (*Welsh* aber'səxan)
Abert 'eɪbɜ:t

1

Figure 2 *Extract B: English Pronouncing Dictionary,* Daniel Jones, Revised by A C Gimson, Cambridge University Press (1991)

Figure 2 *Extract C: Concise Oxford Dictionary.* (Oxford University Press): please see page 14.

A, a[1] [eɪ] **1** *n* **(a)** (*letter*) A, a *m*. **to know sth from A to Z** connaître qch à fond *or* par cœur; **he doesn't know A from B** il est ignare; (*in house numbers*) **24a** 24 bis; (*Brit Aut*) **on the A4** sur la (route) A4, ≃ sur la RN4 *or* la nationale 4.
(b) (*Mus*) la *m*.
2 *cpd*: **A-1,** (*US*) **A no. 1** de première qualité, parfait, champion*; **ABC** *V* **ABC**; **A-bomb** bombe *f* atomique; (*Brit Scol*) **A-levels** ≃ baccalauréat *m*; **A-line dress** robe *f* trapèze *inv*.

a[2] [eɪ, ə] *indef art* (*before vowel or mute h*: **an**) **(a)** un, une. **~ tree** un arbre; **an apple** une pomme; **such ~ hat** un tel *or* pareil chapeau; **so large ~ country** un si grand pays.
(b) (*def art in French*) le, la, les. **to have ~ good ear** avoir l'oreille juste; **he smokes ~ pipe** il fume la pipe; **to set an example** donner l'exemple; **I have read ~ third of the book** j'ai lu le tiers du livre; **we haven't ~ penny** nous n'avons pas le sou; **~ woman hates violence** les femmes détestent la violence.
(c) (*absent in French*) **she was ~ doctor** elle était médecin; **as ~ soldier** en tant que soldat; **my uncle, ~ sailor** mon oncle, qui est marin; **what ~ pleasure!** quel plaisir!; **to make ~ fortune** faire fortune.
(d) un(e) certain(e). **I have heard of ~ Mr X** j'ai entendu parler d'un certain M X.
(e) le *or* la même. **they are much of an age** ils sont du même âge; **they are of ~ size** ils sont de la même grandeur.
(f) (*a single*) un(e) seul(e). **to empty a glass at ~ draught** vider un verre d'un trait; **at ~ blow** d'un seul coup.
(g) (*with abstract nouns*) du, de la, des. **to make ~ noise/~ fuss** faire du bruit/des histoires.
(h) **~ few survivors** quelques survivants; **~ lot of** *or* **~ great many flowers** beaucoup de fleurs.
(i) (*distributive use*) **£4 ~ person/head** 4 livres par personne/par tête; **3 francs ~ kilo** 3 F le kilo; **twice ~ month** deux fois par mois; **twice ~ year** deux fois l'an *or* par an; **80 km an hour** 80 km/h, 80 kilomètres-heure, 80 kilomètres à l'heure.

Aachen ['ɑːxən] *n* Aix-la-Chapelle.

aback [ə'bæk] *adv*: **to be taken ~** être interloqué *or* décontenancé, en rester tout interdit *or* déconcerté.

abacus ['æbəkəs] *n, pl* **abaci** ['æbəsaɪ] **(a)** boulier *m* (compteur), abaque *m*. **(b)** (*Archit*) abaque *m*.

abaft [ə'bɑːft] (*Naut*) **1** *adv* sur *or* vers l'arrière. **2** *prep* en arrière de, sur l'arrière de.

abandon [ə'bændən] **1** *vt* **(a)** (*forsake*) *person* abandonner, quitter, délaisser. (*fig*) **to ~ o.s. to** se livrer à, s'abandonner à, se laisser aller à.
(b) (*Jur etc: give up*) *property, right* renoncer à; *action* se désister de.
(c) (*Naut*) *ship* évacuer; (*Jur*) *cargo* faire (acte de) délaissement de.
2 *n* (*U*) laisser-aller *m*, abandon *m*, relâchement *m*. **with (gay) ~** avec (une belle) désinvolture.

abandoned [ə'bændənd] *adj* **(a)** (*forsaken*) *person* abandonné, délaissé; *place* abandonné. **(b)** (*dissolute*) débauché.

abandonment [ə'bændənmənt] *n* (*lit, fig*) abandon *m*; (*Jur*) *[action]* désistement *m*; *[property, right]* cession *f*; *[cargo]* délaissement *m*.

abase [ə'beɪs] *vt* (*humiliate*) *person* mortifier, humilier; (*degrade*) *person* abaisser, avilir; *person's qualities, actions* rabaisser, ravaler. **to ~ o.s. so far as to do** s'abaisser *or* s'humilier jusqu'à faire.

abasement [ə'beɪsmənt] *n* (*U*) (*moral decay*) dégradation *f*, avilissement *m*; (*humiliation*) humiliation *f*, mortification *f*.

abash [ə'bæʃ] *vt* confondre, décontenancer. **to feel ~ed** être confus.

abate [ə'beɪt] **1** *vi [storm, emotions, pain]* s'apaiser, se calmer; *[flood]* baisser; *[fever]* baisser, décroître; *[wind]* tomber; (*Naut*) mollir; *[courage]* faiblir, s'affaiblir, diminuer; *[rent]* baisser.
2 *vt* **(a)** (*lessen*) affaiblir; *noise, pollution* réduire; (*remove*) supprimer; *rent, tax* baisser.
(b) (*Jur: abolish*) *writ* annuler; *sentence* remettre; *corruption* faire cesser, mettre fin à.

abatement [ə'beɪtmənt] *n* (*U*) (*reduction, lessening*) diminution *f*, réduction *f*; *[noise, pollution]* suppression *f*, réduction; (*Med*) *[illness]* régression *f*; (*Jur*) *[legacy]* réduction; *[punishment]* atténuation *f*; *[fine]* annulation *f*, levée *f*.

abattoir ['æbətwɑːʳ] *n* abattoir *m*.

abbess ['æbɪs] *n* abbesse *f*.

abbey ['æbɪ] *n* (*monastery*) abbaye *f*; (*church*) (église *f*) abbatiale *f*. **Westminster A~** l'Abbaye de Westminster.

abbot ['æbət] *n* abbé *m*, (Père *m*) supérieur *m*.

abbreviate [ə'briːvɪeɪt] *vt* abréger, raccourcir.

abbreviation [əˌbriːvɪ'eɪʃən] *n* abréviation *f*.

ABC ['eɪbiː'siː] *n* abc *m*, alphabet *m*. (*Brit Rail*) **the ~ (guide)** l'indicateur *m* des chemins de fer; **it's as easy** *or* **simple as ~** * c'est simple comme bonjour, rien de plus simple.

abdicate ['æbdɪkeɪt] **1** *vt right* renoncer à, abdiquer; *function* se démettre de. **to ~ the throne** renoncer à la couronne, abdiquer. **2** *vi* abdiquer.

abdication [ˌæbdɪ'keɪʃən] *n [king]* abdication *f*, renonciation *f*; *[mandate etc]* démission *f* (*of* de); *[right]* renonciation (*of* à), désistement *m* (*of* de).

abdomen ['æbdəmen, (*Med*) æb'dəʊmen] *n* abdomen *m*.

abdominal [æb'dɒmɪnl] *adj* abdominal.

abduct [æb'dʌkt] *vt* enlever (*un enfant etc*).

abduction [æb'dʌkʃən] *n* **(a)** (*Jur etc*) enlèvement *m*, rapt *m*. **(b)** (*Logic*) abduction *f*.

abductor [æb'dʌktəʳ] *n* **(a)** (*person*) ravisseur *m*, -euse *f*. **(b)** (*Anat*) abducteur *m*.

abed† [ə'bed] *adv* (*liter*) au lit, couché. **to lie ~** être couché.

aberrant [ə'berənt] *adj* (*Bio, fig*) aberrant, anormal.

aberration [ˌæbə'reɪʃən] *n* **(a)** (*U: lit, fig*) aberration *f*, égarement *m*. **in a moment of ~** dans un moment d'aberration.
(b) (*instance of this*) anomalie *f*, idée *or* action aberrante, aberration *f*.
(c) (*Astron, Opt*) aberration *f*.

abet [ə'bet] *vt* encourager, soutenir. **to ~ sb in a crime** encourager *or* aider qn à commettre un crime; *V* **aid 2**.

abetter, abettor [ə'betəʳ] *n* instigateur *m*, -trice *f* d'un crime.

abeyance [ə'beɪəns] *n* suspension *f* temporaire, interruption *f* provisoire. *[law, custom]* **to fall into ~** tomber en désuétude; **the question is in ~** la question reste en suspens.

abhor [əb'hɔːʳ] *vt* abhorrer, avoir en horreur, exécrer; *V* **nature**.

abhorrence [əb'hɒrəns] *n* horreur *f*, aversion *f* (*of* de), répulsion *f*. **to hold in ~** avoir horreur de, avoir en horreur.

abhorrent [əb'hɒrənt] *adj* odieux, exécrable, répugnant (*to* à).

abide [ə'baɪd] **1** *vt* **(a)** (*neg only: tolerate*) endurer, supporter, souffrir. **I can't ~ her** je ne peux pas la supporter *or* la souffrir *or* la sentir*.
(b) (*liter: await*) attendre.
2 *vi* (†: *endure*) subsister, durer, se maintenir; (*live*) demeurer, habiter.
abide by *vt fus rule, decision* se soumettre à, se conformer à, respecter; *consequences* accepter, supporter; *promise* rester *or* demeurer fidèle à; *resolve* maintenir, s'en tenir à.

abiding [ə'baɪdɪŋ] *adj* (*liter*) constant, éternel; *V* **law** *etc*.

ability [ə'bɪlɪtɪ] *n* **(a)** (*U: power, proficiency*) aptitude *f* (*to do* à faire), capacité *f* (*to do* pour faire), compétence *f* (*in* en, *to do* pour faire). **to the best of one's ~** de son mieux.
(b) (*U: cleverness*) habileté *f*, talent *m*. **a person of great ~** une personne très douée; **he has a certain artistic ~** il a un certain don *or* talent artistique.
(c) (*mental powers*) **abilities** talents *mpl*, dons intellectuels.

abject ['æbdʒekt] *adj person, action* abject, vil, méprisable; *state, condition* misérable, pitoyable; *apology* servile. **in ~ poverty** dans la misère noire.

abjectly ['æbdʒektlɪ] *adv* (*V* **abject**) abjectement; misérablement; avec servilité.

abjure [əb'dʒʊəʳ] *vt one's rights* renoncer (publiquement *or* par serment) à. **to ~ one's religion** abjurer sa religion, apostasier.

ablative ['æblətɪv] **1** *n* ablatif *m*. **in the ~** à l'ablatif; **~ absolute** ablatif absolu. **2** *adj* ablatif.

ablaze [ə'bleɪz] *adv, adj* (*lit*) en feu, en flammes. **to set ~** embraser (*liter*); **to be ~** flamber; (*fig*) **~ with anger** enflammé de colère; (*fig*) **~ with light** resplendissant de lumière.

able ['eɪbl] **1** *adj* **(a)** (*'to be ~ ' sert d'infinitif à l'auxiliaire de mode 'can/could' dans quelques-uns des sens de cet auxiliaire*) **to be ~ to do** (*have means or opportunity*) pouvoir faire; (*know how to*) savoir faire; (*be capable of*) être à même de *or* en mesure de faire; **I ran fast and so was ~ to catch the bus** en courant vite j'ai réussi à attraper l'autobus (*NB 'could' ne peut être employé dans ce contexte*); *V* **can**[1] **b**.
(b) (*having power, means, opportunity*) capable, en état (*to do* de faire), apte, propre (*to do* à faire). **~ to pay** en mesure de payer; **you are better ~ to do it than he is** (*it's easier for you*) vous êtes mieux à même de le faire *or* plus en état de le faire que lui; (*you're better qualified*) vous êtes plus propre à le faire *or* mieux désigné pour le faire que lui.
(c) (*clever*) capable, compétent, de talent. **an ~ man** un homme de talent.

1

Figure 2 *Extract D: Collins-Robert French-English/English-French Dictionary.*

What three things set *Extract A* apart from all the others? To answer this, consider carefully the words it includes and excludes.

Three things set it apart. Firstly, this extract excludes all words not related to architecture. Secondly, this extract includes two people's names (the names of architects), something that most dictionaries would avoid. Thirdly, it contains an illustration.

The next questions deal with *Extracts B, C* and *D.*

a List the sort of information each extract tells you about words. Use my list at the beginning of this unit (p.13) as a guide, and spend only ten minutes on this at most.

Note: the strange script being used for the entries in *Extract B* is phonetic script. It is designed to represent exactly how people say words.

b Underline, in your list, the sort of information *Extracts B, C* and *D* each seem to specialise in.

Extract B

Extract C

Extract D

(continued opposite)

c List your own reasons for consulting a dictionary, in rough order of frequency.

d By comparing your answer to c with your answers to a and b, decide which of these four dictionaries you would choose to have by you most of the time.

Some of the questions are difficult, and you may not agree with me on all points. But here are my attempts at answers.

Question a

The list at the beginning of this unit gives the answer for *Extract C.*

For *Extract B*, I listed:

- some grammatical information (e.g. 'indefinite article');
- pronunciation (a lot is on this);
- spelling;
- history, because we are told where some of the words come from.

For *Extract D*, I listed:

- grammar (e.g. 'aback' is an adverb);
- spelling;
- English meanings (only sometimes, as in the case of 'abide');
- French words that mean the same;
- pronunciation.

There isn't anything on the history of words.

Question b

For *Extract B*, I underlined 'pronunciation'.

For *Extract D*, I underlined 'French words that mean the same'.

Extract C was more awkward. I underlined 'meaning'.

Question c

There is no right answer to this. My own reasons, in order of frequency, were:

- spelling;
- meaning;
- history of the word;
- pronunciation.

I very rarely use a dictionary for other reasons.

Question d

I chose *Extract C.*

Your answers to these questions, when you look at them together, should bring home some vital points. These are, firstly, that none of these four books is perfect. All omit important information about the words they list, and *Extract A* omits many words. Secondly, the general dictionary (*Extract C*) is probably the best choice for reference most of the time, but it fails to give you very important information that the other books include. It is not as good as *B* on pronunciation, or as *A* on architectural terms, and doesn't even try to compete with *D* on French translation. If you want more than it offers in each of these areas, you would be better off with a suitable specialist dictionary. However, none of these specialist dictionaries would be much good outside its own field of information.

This book will be about general dictionaries, and we will have plenty to study in these alone. But the basic point about them has to be made clear. Any portable general dictionary is a compromise between thoroughness, clarity, brevity and cost. At times you will find out that yours can't tell you what you want to know. When this happens you may be able to solve your difficulty by consulting a bigger general dictionary in a library, or at home if you have one there. But you must never forget the specialist volumes. If you really want to look up everything about, for example, the history of a word, the appropriate specialist book (an etymological dictionary) will be a better bet than any general dictionary you are likely to find. Also, if you are really interested in a subject, whether it is architecture, linguistics or sociology, a short specialist dictionary will be very useful. Your local library may have one. If not, it may well be worth your while to buy one.

Different sizes of general dictionary

After all this, you may feel that there are no more complications to face before we get down to our chosen dictionary. However, there is one more. I have just said that 'Any portable general dictionary is a compromise between thoroughness, clarity, brevity and cost'. You need to remember that they don't all make the same compromise. Partly, of course, this is to do with questions of size and cost, but there is more to it than that. Big, complicated dictionaries are not suitable for some sorts of use, even if they're to hand. To take an extreme case, what good is the *Oxford English Dictionary* to nine year olds? They will find out nothing from it. They need a dictionary that is very clear indeed, gives examples, concentrates on meanings, and only lists the 'hard' words. And adults, writing essays at college or at home, will find that what they require is quite a small dictionary for straightforward checking of spellings and basic meanings, as short, simpler books are usually easier to find things in. These are not just cheap and pocket-sized; they are actually better for quick reference. Indeed, each size of general dictionary is suited to a different job.

This point only becomes really clear when you look at examples. So please read carefully the extracts in *Figure 3.* Then attempt the following SAQ.

a Put the extracts in order of increasing complexity.

b Ignoring questions of cost and of probable size, decide which dictionary would be your choice:

- to be beside you when you are writing a letter or essay;
- to be up on a shelf at home for reference when you hit real problems;
- to be kept in a library for puzzled members of the public to consult when their own dictionaries let them down.

Figure 3 *Extract A: Concise Oxford Dictionary:* please see page 14.

a *or* **A** (eɪ) *n.*, *pl.* **a's, A's,** *or* **As. 1.** the first letter of the English alphabet. **2.** the first in a series. **3. from A to Z.** from start to finish.

a (ə; *emphatic* eɪ) *det.* (*indefinite article;* used before an initial consonant. Compare **an**) **1.** used preceding a singular countable noun that has not been mentioned before: *a dog; a great pity.* **2.** used preceding a noun or determiner of quantity: *a dozen eggs; a great many; to read a lot.* **3.** (preceded by *once, twice, several times,* etc.) each or every; per: *once a day.*

A 1. *Music.* the sixth note of the scale of C major. **2.** ampere(s). **3.** atomic: *an A-bomb.*

Å angstrom unit.

A. answer.

a- *or before a vowel* **an-** *prefix.* not; without: *atonal; asocial; anaphrodisiac.* [Greek]

A1, A-1, *or* **A-one** (ˈeɪˈwʌn) *adj. Informal.* first-class; excellent.

A4 *n.* a standard paper size, 297 × 210 mm.

AA 1. Alcoholics Anonymous. **2.** (in Britain) Automobile Association.

AAA (ˈθriːˈeɪz) *Brit.* Amateur Athletic Association.

A & R artists and repertoire.

aardvark (ˈɑːdˌvɑːk) *n.* an African mammal which has long ears and snout and which feeds on termites. [obs. Afrikaans: earth pig]

AB able-bodied seaman.

ab- *prefix.* away from; opposite to: *abnormal.* [Latin]

aback (əˈbæk) *adv.* **taken aback.** startled or disconcerted.

abacus (ˈæbəkəs) *n.* **1.** a counting device consisting of a frame holding rods on which beads are moved backwards and forwards by the person doing the counting. **2.** *Archit.* the flat upper part of the capital of a column. [Greek, from Hebrew]

abaft (əˈbɑːft) *adv., adj. Naut.* closer to the stern of a ship. [Old English *be* by + *æftan* behind]

abalone (ˌæbəˈləʊnɪ) *n.* an edible sea creature with an ear-shaped shell lined with mother-of-pearl. [American Spanish]

abandon (əˈbændən) *vb.* **1.** to leave (someone or something): *he abandoned his wife.* **2.** to give up completely: *abandon hope.* **3.** to surrender (oneself) to emotion without restraint. ~*n.* **4.** freedom from inhibitions or restraint. [Old French *a bandon* under one's control] —**aˈbandonment** *n.*

abandoned (əˈbændənd) *adj.* **1.** deserted: *an abandoned windmill.* **2.** uninhibited: *abandoned behaviour.*

abase (əˈbeɪs) *vb.* **abase oneself.** to degrade oneself. [Old French *abaissier*] —**aˈbasement** *n.*

abashed (əˈbæʃt) *adj.* embarrassed and ashamed. [Old French *esbair* to be astonished]

abate (əˈbeɪt) *vb.* to make or become less strong: *the storm abated.* [Old French *abatre* to beat down] —**aˈbatement** *n.*

abattoir (ˈæbəˌtwɑː) *n.* a slaughterhouse. [French *abattre* to fell]

abbacy (ˈæbəsɪ) *n., pl.* **-cies.** the office or jurisdiction of an abbot or abbess. [Church Latin *abbātia*]

abbé (ˈæbeɪ) *n.* a French abbot or other clergyman.

abbess (ˈæbɪs) *n.* the female superior of a convent. [Church Latin *abbātissa*]

abbey (ˈæbɪ) *n.* **1.** a building inhabited by monks or nuns. **2.** a church associated with such a building. **3.** a community of monks or nuns. [Church Latin *abbātia* ABBACY]

abbot (ˈæbət) *n.* the superior of an abbey of monks. [Aramaic *abbā* father]

abbreviate (əˈbriːvɪˌeɪt) *vb.* **1.** to shorten (a word) by omission of some letters **2.** to cut short. [Latin *brevis* brief] —**abbreviation** (əˌbriːvɪˈeɪʃən) *n.*

ABC *n.* **1.** the alphabet. **2.** an alphabetical guide.

abdicate (ˈæbdɪˌkeɪt) *vb.* **1.** to give up the throne formally. **2.** to give up (one's responsibilities). [Latin *abdicāre* to disclaim] —**ˌabdiˈcation** *n.*

abdomen (ˈæbdəmən) *n.* the part of the body that contains the stomach and intestines; belly. [Latin] —**abdominal** (æbˈdɒmɪnˀl) *adj.*

abduct (æbˈdʌkt) *vb.* to remove (a person) by force; kidnap. [Latin *abdūcere* to lead away] —**abˈduction** *n.* —**abˈductor** *n.*

abeam (əˈbiːm) *adv., adj.* at right angles to the length of a vessel or aircraft.

Aberdeen Angus (ˈæbədiːn ˈæŋgəs) *n.* a black hornless breed of beef cattle originating in Scotland.

aberrant (əˈbɛrənt) *adj.* deviating from what is right, true, or normal.

aberration (ˌæbəˈreɪʃən) *n.* **1.** deviation from what is right, true, or normal **2.** a lapse: *a mental aberration.* [Latin *aberrāre* to wander away]

abet (əˈbɛt) *vb.* **abetting, abetted.** to assist or encourage (someone) in wrongdoing. [Old French *abeter* to lure on]

abeyance (əˈbeɪəns) *n.* (usually preceded by *in* or *into*) a state of being put aside temporarily. [Old French *abeance,* lit.: a gaping after]

abhor (əbˈhɔː) *vb.* **-horring, -horred.** to detest (something) vehemently. [Latin *abhorrēre*]

abhorrent (əbˈhɒrənt) *adj.* hateful; loathsome. —**abˈhorrence** *n.*

Figure 3 *Extract B: Collins New Compact English Dictionary.* (HarperCollins) 2nd Edition, 1989

A (ē[i]), the first letter of the Roman and English Alphabet (Gr. *Alpha*, Heb. *Aleph*); repr. orig. in Eng., as in L., the 'low-back-wide' vowel, formed with the widest opening of jaws, pharynx, and lips. Pl. *aes*, A's, *A*s.

For its principal sounds see KEY TO THE PRONUNCIATION.

II. Besides serial order, *A* or *a* signifies *spec.* **1.** *Mus.* The 6th note of the diatonic scale of C major, or the first of the relative minor scale of C. Also, the scale of a composition with A as its key-note. **2.** *Naut.* See A 1 below. **3.** In *Logic*: a universal affirmative. **4.** In *Law*, *reasoning*, etc.: any one thing or person. **5.** In *Algebra*: *a*, *b*, *c*, etc., stand for known quantities, *x*, *y*, *z* for unknown.

III. *Abbreviations*. A., a., *a*. = **1.** *anno*, as A.D. *anno domini*, in the year of our Lord; A.M. *anno mundi*, in the year of the world; A.U.C. *anno urbis conditæ*, in the year of the founding of the City (Rome). **2.** *ante*, as a.m. *ante meridiem*, before noon; a. or *a* 1600. **3.** *adjective*; *active* (verb). **4.** *artium*, as A.B. (= B.A.) *artium baccalaureus*, A.M. (= M.A.) *artium magister*, Bachelor, and Master, of Arts. **5.** *alto*. **6.** *accepted* (of bills). **7.** *Associate*, as A.L.S. Associate of the Linnean Society. **8.** R.A. Royal Artillery, Academy, or Academician; F.B.A. Fellow of the British Academy; F.S.A. Fellow of the Society of Antiquaries. **9.** A.B. able-bodied seaman. **10.** *ā* or *āā* in Med. ANA, q.v. **11.** A.C. or a.c., alternating current.

IV. *Phrases*. **1. A per se**, A by itself, *esp.* as a word; hence *fig.* (also † **Apersie**, † **Apersey**, † **A per C**) the first, best, or unique person or thing; = mod. *A* 1. **2.** A 1. Used of ships in first-class condition, as to hull (A), and stores (1). (Lloyd's Register.) Hence *colloq.* *A* 1, U.S. *A No.* 1 = prime, first-class, e.g. An A number one cook MRS. STOWE.

† **A**, *adj.*[1] definite numeral. *Obs.* or *dial.* [OE. *ān*, one, later *ā* bef. a cons., became in the south *on* (*oon*, *one*), *o* (*oo*) and finally *one*; *an* and *a* becoming the 'indef. article'. See next wd. In the north *an(e* and *a* had both senses.] See AN(E, O *a.*, and ONE.

A (toneless ă, ə; emph. ēi), *adj.*[2], called 'indefinite article'. Bef. a vowel-sound **an** (ăn, emph. æn). A weakening of OE. *ān*, 'one', which, *c* 1150, became proclitic and toneless, ăn, ă; see prec. wd. *An* is freq. bef. a cons. to 1300, bef. sounded *h* till after 1700. Now *an* is used bef. a vowel-sound or *h* mute; *a* bef. a cons., sounded *h*, and *eu-*, *u-* pronounced iu, iū, as *a host*, *a eunuch*, *a unit*. But in *unaccented* syllables, many writers retain *an* bef. sounded *h*, some bef. *eu*, *u*, as *an historian*, *an university*. About the 15th cent. *a* or *an* was commonly joined with its sb. as *aman*, *anadder*, *anewt*. Hence, by mistaken division, words like ADDER, NEWT. *A* is strictly *adjective*, and requires a sb. Meanings:—**1.** One, some, any ME. **2.** *A* with numeral adjectives = some, a matter of, about OE. **3.** A certain, a particular ME. **4.** The same 1551. **5.** In each, to or for each. This was orig. the prep. *a*, OE. *an*, *on*, defining time, as in twice *a* day; afterwards identified with the 'indef. art.', and extended from time to space, measure, weight, number. See A *prep.*[1]

1. A tree, a wish, an ice, a pouring rain (*mod.*) A Daniel SHAKS. A Poland TENNYSON. Also, following the adj. preceded by *how*, *so*, *as*, *too*, and in *many a*, *such a*, *what a!* Ho, such a one! *Ruth* 4:1. Behold, how great a matter a little fire kindleth *James* 3:5. What manner a man = *cujusmodi homo?* As fine a child as you shall see (*mod.*). Appar. bef. pl. nouns (*of* omitted): A dozen (of) men. A certayne noble knightis .. she kept LD. BERNERS. Poore a thousand crownes *A.Y.L.* I. i. 2. More than a dozen times TYNDALL. **2.** A ii hundred speres LD. BERNERS. And a many merry men with him *A.Y.L.* I. i. 121. *Obs.* except in *a few*, *a great many*, *a good many*, and in dial. **3.** Phr. *Once on a time*. **4.** These foyles have all a length *Haml.* v. ii. 277. *Mod.* Fowls of a feather. Two at a time. **5.** A peny a daye TINDALE *Matt.* 20:2. Twentie poundes a bowe 1584. Four pieces of eight a man DE FOE. A penny a mile, sixpence a pound (*mod.*).

A, also **a'** (ǫ), *adj.*[3] [From ALL; *l* lost as in *alms*, *talk*; *a'* is the current sp. in modern literary Scotch.] = ALL.

† **A** (ă), *pron. Obs.* or *dial.* [for HA = HE, HEO, HI, *he* (*Haml.* III. iii. 74), *she* (*it*), *they*, when stressless, chiefly in S. and W.] ME.

† **A**, *v.* for **ha, ha'**, worn down f. HAVE (cf. Fr. *a* = L. *habet*). Frequent in 13–17th c.; since, chiefly *colloq.* or *dial.* (TENNYSON *Northern Farmer*), and usu. spelt *ha*, *ha'*.

† **A**, *adv.* Also **aa, o, oo.** [OE. *ā*, *āwa*, replaced in 13th c. by Norse *aȝ*, *ai*, *ei*, *ay*, *aye*. See AYE and O.] Ever, always.

A (ă), *prep.*[1], also **o.** [Worn down proclitic f. OE. prep. *an*, *on*. Now repl. by *on*, *in*, etc., exc. in phr. like *go a begging*, etc., and in compounds like *abed*, *alive*, *asleep*, etc.] **1.** Superposition: on; as *a bed*, etc. ME. **2.** Motion: on, upon, on to; as *a field*, etc. ME. **3.** Juxtaposition: on, at; as in *a right* (or *left*) *half* ME. † **4.** Position or situation: in; as *a Rome* –1660. **5.** Direction or position: towards; as *a back*, etc. ME. **6.** Partition: in, into; as *a pieces* ME. † **7.** Position in a series: at, in; as *a first*, etc. ME. **8.** Time: in, on, by; as *a night* OE. With OE. genitives *a nights*, *nowadays*. Esp. with advbs. of repetition: *once a day* (OE. *on dæȝe*). See A *adj.*[2] 5, and cf. Fr. *deux francs par jour*. † **9.** Manner: in, with, etc.; as *a this wise*, *a purpose* = on purpose –1695. † **10.** Capacity: in any one's name, esp. *a God's name* –1702. **11.** State: in; as *a live*, etc. ME. **12.** Process: in course of; as in *whilst these things were a doing* STOW. ME. In mod.Eng. *were doing*, *were being done*. **13.** Action; **a.** with *be*: engaged in; as in *They had ben a fyghtyng* LD. BERNERS. Mod., *been fighting*. **b.** with vb. of motion: as in *to go a begging*, etc. ME.

† **A** (ă, ə), *prep.*[2] ME. [Worn down from *of*, and once used for it in *men a war*, *time a day*, etc.] **1.** Of, *esp.* in *a clock* = of the clock. **2.** After *manner*, *kind*, *sort*, etc., *of* in its reduced form was identified with the 'indef. art.'; thus, What manner of man? *cujusmodi homo?* became 'what manner a man?'

1. Cloth a gold *Much Ado* III. iv. 19. It's sixe a clock B. JONS. **2.** No maner a person LD. BERNERS.

† **A**, *conj.* ME. [Occurs before a consonant for *an*; see AN, AN', *conj.*] **1.** = And. **2.** = And, an', if.

† **A**, *interj.* ME. [var. of O, AH.] **1.** O! exclam. of surprise, admiration. **2.** Ah! of grief. **3.** Before proper names as a war-cry, as *A Warwick!* **4.** As in *merrily hent the Stile-a* SHAKS., for metre; now burlesque. Cf. O! as in 'My Nannie, O'.

A, a- (ă, ə) *particle* or *prefix*, reduced form (now s.w. dial.) of I-[1], Y-, the prefix of pa. pples. late ME.

An' we have all a-left the spot W. BARNES.

A-, *prefix*. **1.** OE. **a-**, orig. *ar-* away, on, up, out, as in *a-rise*. Sometimes confused with OFr. *a-* :- L. *ad-*, *ac-*, *af-*, etc., as in *a(c)-curse*, etc. **2.** ME. **a-** :- OE. *an*, *on*, in, on, engaged in, at, as in *asleep*, etc. See A *prep.*[1] **3.** ME. **a-** :- OE. *of* prep. off, from, of, as in *akin*, etc. See A *prep.*[2] **4.** ME. **a-** :- OE. *and-*, against, opposite, as in *a-long*. **5.** ME. **a-** for AT, as in *ado*, early N. Eng. *at do* = inf. *to do*. **6. a-** for *i-*, *y-* :- *ȝe-*; see A *particle*. **7.** ME. **a-** = Fr. pref. *a-* :- L. *ad-* to, at, expressing addition, increase, change *into*. In 15th c., as in Fr., most words from OFr. with (and some without) this prefix were treated as if formed directly from L. Cf. *a(d)dress*, *a(f)fect*, *a(c)curse* = OE. *a-* + *curse*. **8.** ME. **a-** = Fr. *a-* :- L. *ab* off, away, from, as in *a-soil*. **9.** ME. **a-** = AFr. *a*, OFr. *e-*, *es-* :- L. *ex-* out, utterly, as in *abash*. **10.** ME. **a-** :- AFr. *an-*, OFr. *en-*, as in *abushment*, etc. **11.** *a-*, as used by Spenser and others, is often due to vague form-association only. **12. a-**, f. L. *a* = *ad*, to, reduced to *a-* bef. *sc-*, *sp-*, *st-*, as in *a-scend*, etc. See AD-. **13. a-**, f. L. *a* = *ab* from, off, away; only bef. *v*, as in *avert*; see AB-. **14. a-**, f. Gr. ἀ- used bef. a cons. for ἀν = *without*, *not*, *-less* as in *adamant*, *apetalous*, etc. In *agnostic*, etc., *a-* = *un-*, *non-*, and is used also with techn. words from L., as *a-sexual*.

-a, *suffix*. **1.** OE. **-a** (:- Gmc., *-on*), nom. ending, as in *ox-a* = ME. *ox-e*, mod.E. *ox*. A com. ending of OE. names and titles, as *Bæda*. **2.** Gr. and L. **-a**, nom. ending of fem. nouns (*esp.* Nat. Hist. terms, and names of women), often adopted unchanged, as *idea*, *soda*, *Diana*, etc. **3.** Mod. Rom. **-a**, ending of fem. nouns, names of women, and occ. a sex-suffix, as *stanza*; *Eva*; *donn-a*, etc. **4.** Gr. and L. **-a**, pl. ending of neut. nouns, occ. adopted unchanged, as *data*, *Mammalia*, etc.

‖ **Aal** (āl). 1875. [Hind.] A species of *Morinda*, whose roots yield a red dye. Also, the dye.

‖ **Aam** (ām, ǫm). 1526. [Du. *aam*, = G. *ahm*, *ohm*, – (ult.) Gr. ἄμη bucket.] A Du. and Ger. liquid measure, varying from 37 to 41 gallons; a cask.

‖ **Aard-vark** (ā·ɹdvāɹk). 1833. [S. Afr. Du., f. *aarde* earth + *vark* pig.] An insectivorous quadruped (*Orycteropus capensis*), one of the Edentata, intermediate between Armadillos and Ant-eaters.

‖ **Aard-wolf** (ā·ɹdwulf). 1833. [S. Afr. Du., f. *aarde* earth + *wolf* wolf.] A S. Afr. carnivorous quadruped (*Proteles lalandii*), intermediate between the dogs, hyenas, and civets.

Aaronic, -al (eᵊrǫ·nik, -ăl), *a.* 1874. [f. the prop. name; see -IC, -ICAL.] Pertaining to Aaron, Levitical, high-priestly.

Aaron's-beard (ēᵊ·rənzbīᵊ·ɹd). 1549. [*Ps.* 133:2.] *Herb.* A name, *esp.* of the Great St. John's wort (*Hypericum calycinum*), and locally of other plants.

Aaron's rod. 1834. **1.** [*Num.* 17:8.] *Herb.* A name of plants, *esp.* the Great Mullein or Hag-taper (*Verbascum thapsus*), and the Golden Rod (*Solidago virgaurea*). **2.** [*Exod.* 7:9.] *Arch.* A rod with a serpent twined about it, used as an ornament.

‖ **Ab** (æb). 1833. [Heb.] The 5th month of the Heb. sacred year, the 11th of the civil year. The 12th month of the Syrian year, = August.

Ab-, *pref.* repr. L. *ab*, 'off, away, from'. In rec. formations, e.g. *ab-oral*, *ab-* = 'position away from'.

Aba (æ·bă). 1876. A new altazimuth instrument, designed by M. d'Abbadie [and named after him] for determining latitude, etc., without the sextant.

‖ **Abaca** (æ·băkă), **-ka.** The native name of the palm (*Musa textilis*) which furnishes Manilla Hemp; also, its fibre.

Abacinate (ăbæ·sineit), *v. rare.* [– *abacinat-*, pa. ppl. stem of med.L. *abacinare*, f. *ab* AB- + *bacinus* BASIN; see -ATE[3].] To blind by placing hot irons or metal plates before the eyes. Hence **Abacina·tion.**

‖ **Abaci·scus.** [L., – Gr. ἀβακίσκος, dim. of ἄβαξ ABACUS.] *Arch.* **1.** A tile or square in a mosaic pavement. † **2.** = ABACUS.

Abacist (æ·băsist). ME. [– med.L. *abacista*, f. L. *abacus*; see -IST.] One who uses an abacus in casting accounts; a calculator.

† **Aback.** *rare.* [– Fr. *abaque* – L. *abacus*.] A square tablet or compartment.

Aback (ăbæ·k), *adv.* [OE. *on* (A *prep.*[1] 5, A- *pref.* 2) + *bæc* BACK *sb.*[1] Now chiefly *Naut.*] **1.** Backwards. Also *fig.* **2.** In the rear, behind OE. Also *fig.* **3.** *Naut.* Of sails: Laid back against the mast, with the wind in

B

Figure 3 *Extract C: Shorter Oxford English Dictionary.* (Oxford University Press) 3rd Edition, 1972

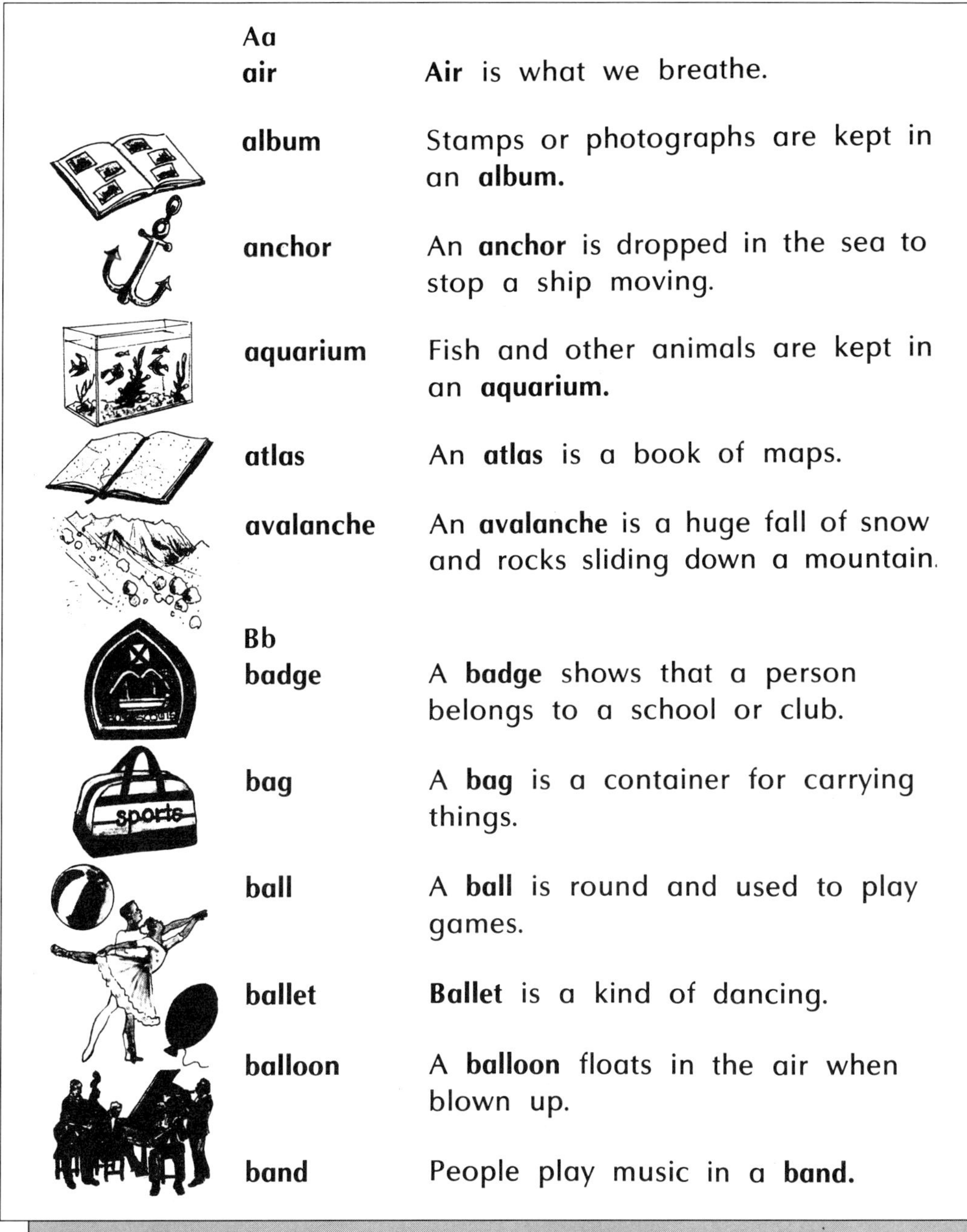

Aa

air — **Air** is what we breathe.

album — Stamps or photographs are kept in an **album.**

anchor — An **anchor** is dropped in the sea to stop a ship moving.

aquarium — Fish and other animals are kept in an **aquarium.**

atlas — An **atlas** is a book of maps.

avalanche — An **avalanche** is a huge fall of snow and rocks sliding down a mountain.

Bb

badge — A **badge** shows that a person belongs to a school or club.

bag — A **bag** is a container for carrying things.

ball — A **ball** is round and used to play games.

ballet — **Ballet** is a kind of dancing.

balloon — A **balloon** floats in the air when blown up.

band — People play music in a **band.**

Figure 3 *Extract D: Dictionary One.* (CollinsEducational)

The correct order of complexity is *D*, *B*, *A*, *C*.

You and I might not agree on the 'correct' answers to Question b. This is an area of personal judgement. I'd want *B* by my side, *A* on the shelf, and *C* in the library.

To study this book further you need a clear general dictionary, portable and inexpensive, containing the basic information that is often all you need. The *Collins New Compact English Dictionary* would be suitable, or any of its competitors, such as *Chambers Pocket English Dictionary* or the *Pocket Oxford Dictionary.*

Before you launch into the units on using such a dictionary, look back for a moment at the last set of extracts. Remind yourself of how the virtues of the child's dictionary – selection of words, brevity, simplicity – are exactly the things that prevent it from being any good as a reference volume for adults. An adult's pocket dictionary, just like a child's, has serious limitations precisely because it is well designed for its job. If you remember that, you won't expect too much of it.

UNIT 3 USING A STANDARD GENERAL DICTIONARY

What this unit is about

By the time you have finished your work on this unit, you should be able to:

- give reasons why a dictionary is set out in the way it is;
- identify, with the help of your dictionary, the nouns, adjectives and verbs from a given list;
- explain the meaning of some of the more important abbreviations used in the dictionary.

Introduction

Some of us have had the experience at school of being told to 'use your dictionary', but we were never shown how; consequently we made rather limited use of it. The trouble is that the early pages in most dictionaries are rather off-putting, written in complex and tightly-packed language and unattractively presented in tiny print, as the example below shows.

2. Pronunciation

2.1 Guidance on pronunciation follows the system of the International Phonetic Alphabet (IPA). Only the pronunciation standard in southern England is given.

2.1.1 *Consonants*:

b, *d*, *f*, *h*, *k*, *l*, *m*, *n*, *p*, *r*, *s*, *t*, *v*, *w*, and *z* have their usual English values. Other symbols are used as follows:

g	(*g*ame)	ŋ	(lo*ng*)	ʃ	(*sh*ip)
tʃ	(*ch*air)	θ	(*th*in)	ʒ	(mea*s*ure)
dʒ	(*j*et)	ð	(*th*ere)	j	(*y*es)
x	(Scots etc.: lo*ch*)				

Yet the introductory pages from which these extracts are taken are of crucial importance. Once you have got to grips with them you will be able to treat your dictionary as a friend rather than as a confusing cluster of unconnected words.

Why the dictionary is laid out as it is

Many readers are put off using a dictionary because it looks so confusing and so unlike most other printed matter met in everyday life. In fact, it is set out in a particular way for good reasons, and the time taken in getting used to the lay-out is time well spent.

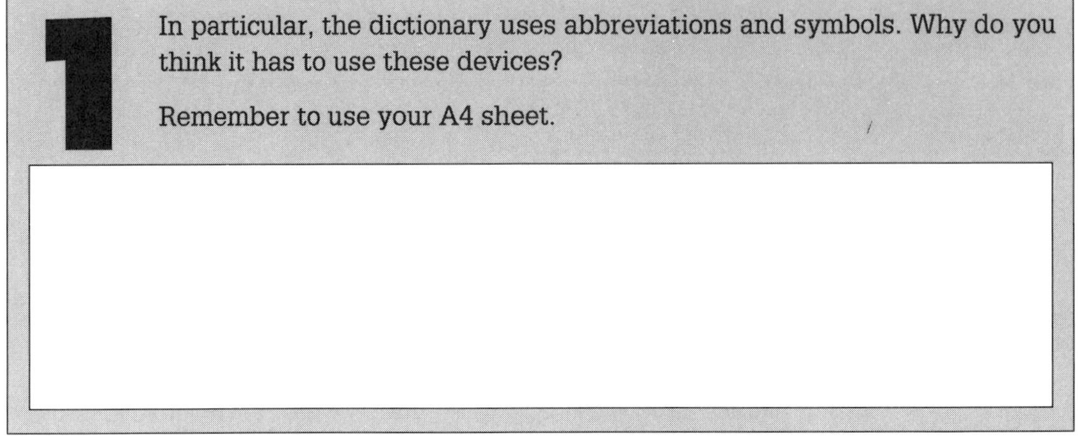

1 In particular, the dictionary uses abbreviations and symbols. Why do you think it has to use these devices?

Remember to use your A4 sheet.

To save space.

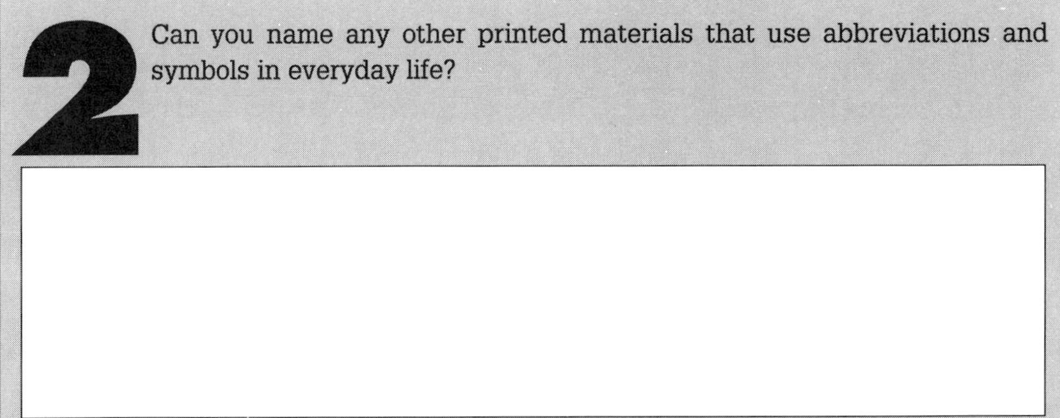

2 Can you name any other printed materials that use abbreviations and symbols in everyday life?

Examples include knitting patterns, do-it-yourself instructions, cookery recipes, road signs. All use abbreviations to save space and to save time.

3 Look at the dictionary entry that follows from the *Collins New Compact*, and at the excerpt from the *AA Members' Handbook*.

a

fuss (fʌs) *n.* **1.** nervous activity or agitation. **2.** complaint or objection: *he made a fuss over the bill.* **3.** an exhibition of affection or admiration: *they made a great fuss over the new baby.* ~*vb.* **4.** to worry unnecessarily. **5.** to be excessively concerned over trifles. **6.** (usually foll. by *over*) to show great or excessive concern or affection (for). **7.** to bother (a person). [origin unknown]

fusspot (ˈfʌsˌpɒt) *n. Brit. informal.* a person who fusses unnecessarily.

fussy (ˈfʌsɪ) *adj.* **fussier, fussiest. 1.** inclined to fuss. **2.** very particular about detail. **3.** overelaborate. —ˈ**fussily** *adv.*

(from *Collins New Compact English Dictionary*)

(continued opposite)

b

STONE 12,203 Staffs (☎0785) Map26SJ93
EcWed MdTue/cattle
★★★**Crown Osprey** High St (TRL)
☎813535 rm13🛁 A:rm16🚿 ✖ 200**P**
★★★**Stone House** ☎815531
rm22(13🛁9🚿) 100**P** B&B*(c-d)*
★★**Mill** Mill St ☎818456 rm10(1🛁5🚿)
108**P** B&B*(a-b)*
APP SP ✪***Robert Simcock & Sons*** Norton
Bridge ☎760281 R18.30 ✾ **B** Rov

(from *AA Members' Handbook*, 1988/89)

Both the dictionary and the handbook use letters to stand for words. Make a list of these. You don't have to say what they stand for, though I explain them in my response. Remember to use your A4 sheet.

There are several. I give a selection below.

a	n.	=	noun
	vb.	=	verb
	foll.	=	followed
	adj.	=	adjective

We can find out what these abbreviations stand for by consulting the relevant *keys*.

b	Map 26S J93	=	a map reference: Stone can be located by looking up this reference on a map elsewhere in the handbook.
	TRL	=	Toby Restaurants Ltd
	rm	=	rooms
	A	=	annexe
	P	=	parking (on hotel premises)
	(c-d)	=	a price range
	APP	=	Appointed Garage
	SP	=	Specialist Appointment
	B	=	Major Body Repairs Specialist
	Rov	=	a franchise holder for Rover Group

(The 'R' before 1830 does not seem to be explained in the handbook key. It probably means 'Repairs and servicing available until the time shown'.)

But both the dictionary and the *AA Members' Handbook* also use visual symbols to represent information in shortened form.

Look first at these drawings from the *AA Members' Handbook* entry on Stone.

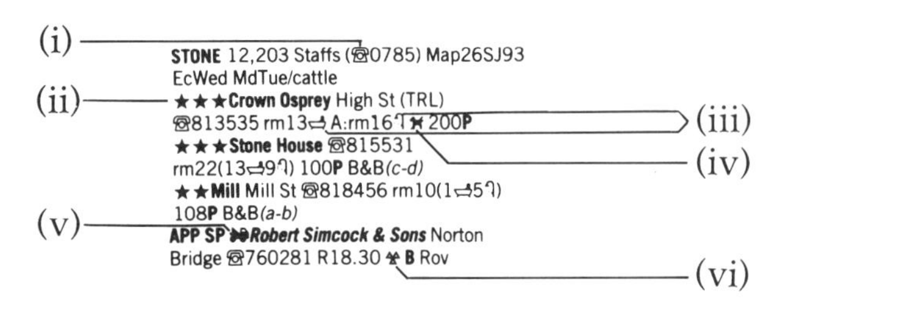

(i) **STONE** 12,203 Staffs (☎0785) Map26SJ93
EcWed MdTue/cattle
(ii) ★★★**Crown Osprey** High St (TRL)
☎813535 rm13⇌ A:rm16⇌ ✗ 200P (iii)
★★★**Stone House** ☎815531
rm22(13⇌9⇌) 100P B&B*(c-d)* (iv)
★★**Mill** Mill St ☎818456 rm10(1⇌5⇌)
108P B&B*(a-b)*
(v) **APP SP** ✱***Robert Simcock & Sons*** Norton
Bridge ☎760281 R18.30 ☢ **B** Rov (vi)

(from *AA Members' Handbook*, 1988/89)

Write down what each of these symbols stands for, by looking at the following key.

ABBREVIATIONS

General Entries

[AA]	AA Centre (see pages 39-42)	
☎	telephone	*unless stated, the name of the exchange is the same as the placename; at hotels the number is usually for reception only*
☎	night telephone	
Ec	early closing	
ex	except	
Map	figures and letters which follow give the service atlas page number and the national grid reference (see Atlas page 1)	
Md	market day	

Hotel Entries

★	hotel classification (see page 44)
★	hotel classification (see page 44)
⌂	lodge classification (see page 44)
○	hotel likely to open during the currency of the *Members' Handbook*
♣	country house hotel (see page 44)
HBL	merit award (see page 44)
✿	rosette award (see page 44)
©	mainly grill-type meals
THF *etc*	abbreviations for hotel groups (see page 46)
C	closed for two months or more within a year
CC	closed for less than two months at any one time
RS	restricted services operate for a period
U	unlicensed
rm	number of bedrooms (see page 45)
⇌	private bathroom and/or shower with own toilet (see page 45)
A	annexe (followed by number of rooms) (see page 45)
✗	no dogs
P	parking on hotel premises (number of cars usually stated)
P	no parking available on hotel premises

nc	no children *eg* nc4 = no children under 4 years of age
B&B	bed and breakfast per single room
B	room rate only per single room

Price-banding System

Price-bands indicate likely charges per single room per night (incl. VAT and service).

Rates for one and two star hotels based on cheapest single room.

Rates for three, four and five star hotels based on cheapest single room with private bath or shower and lavatory.

Where hotel's 1988 price is close to top of band, or where only 1987 price known, next band up also given.

Prices may change during currency of *Members' Handbook*—so always check before booking.

Price-band	Charges
a	up to £20
b	£20 to £25
c	£25 to £30
d	£30 to £35
e	£35 to £45
f	£45 to £55
g	£55 to £80
h	£80 to £100
j	£100 and over

Garage Entries (see page 46)

APP	Appointed Garages
SP	Specialist Appointment
✱	Breakdown Service
(motorcycle symbol)	Motorcycle Repairer
☢	approved vehicle testing station at time of going to press; it is advisable to confirm by telephone
PI	Petrol Injection Specialist
D	Diesel Specialist
E	Electrical & Electronic Specialist
AT	Automatic Transmission Specialist
B	Major Body Repairs Specialist
Vau etc	abbreviations for franchises held by garages

(from *AA Members' Handbook*, 1988/89)

(continued opposite)

This has given you practice in 'looking things up' and this practice will come in very useful when we look at the dictionary again later in this unit. You had to find the right places in the key and this tells you that:

(i) is the symbol for the telephone. (Note that the first time this appears it gives the Stone code, applicable to all the following numbers.)

(ii) gives the hotel classification; you are referred to a separate key for this;

(iii) shows the facilities in rooms (bath/shower). Again, you are referred elsewhere in the handbook for more detail;

(iv) means that no dogs are allowed;

(v) means that this garage operates a breakdown service;

(vi) shows this is an approved vehicle-testing station.

Now look at the entry from the dictionary again. List all the symbols (whether letters or any other kind) you can find. But for the moment ignore the symbols and letters in brackets straight after the first word of each listing. Don't work out their meaning yet – just list them.

fuss (fʌs) *n.* **1.** nervous activity or agitation. **2.** complaint or objection: *he made a fuss over the bill.* **3.** an exhibition of affection or admiration: *they made a great fuss over the new baby.* ~*vb.* **4.** to worry unnecessarily. **5.** to be excessively concerned over trifles. **6.** (usually foll. by *over*) to show great or excessive concern or affection (for). **7.** to bother (a person). [origin unknown]

fusspot ('fʌsˌpɒt) *n. Brit. informal.* a person who fusses unnecessarily.

fussy ('fʌsɪ) *adj.* **fussier, fussiest. 1.** inclined to fuss. **2.** very particular about detail. **3.** overelaborate. —'**fussily** *adv.*

How many of these symbols can you understand or guess at? Jot down your answer so that you can compare it with the explanation given later in this unit.

We have now practised looking up abbreviations to make sure of their meanings. We have seen why books like the *AA Members' Handbook* and the dictionary have to use such symbols and abbreviations: they have to pack a great deal of information into a very limited space. (Imagine how long the *AA Members' Handbook* would be if the meaning of the approved vehicle testing station symbol were printed in full each time!)

But these reference books do expect quite a lot of you, the reader. You have to:

- spend time at the start, mastering the 'code';
- expand the symbols into the right meanings.

If readers of the *AA Members' Handbook* didn't use these two skills they could:

- waste money ringing the wrong telephone numbers;
- waste time in cold, unpleasant conditions;
- lose their temper and upset their waiting family;
- further damage their car.

If you can acquire the skills of good dictionary use, you too will save yourself time, energy, and perhaps even money! So let's turn again to the dictionary entry, and look at the way it is set out.

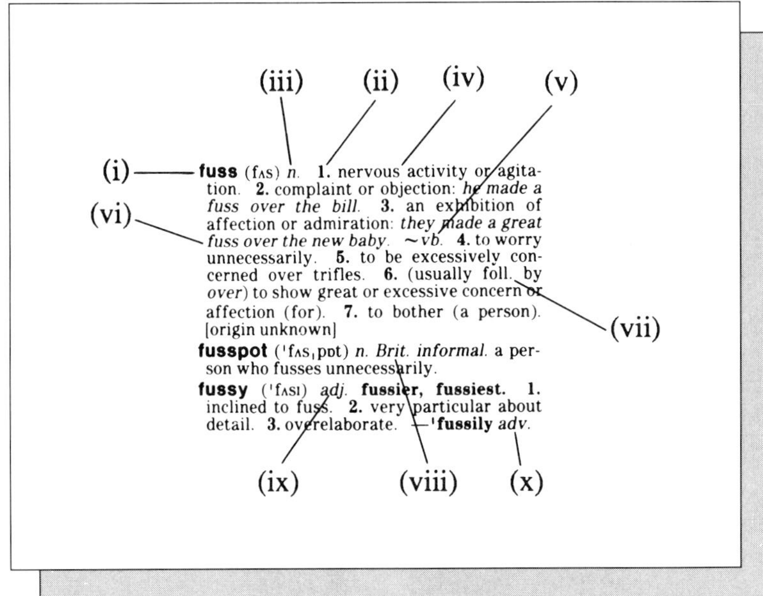

(i) = the word itself (bold type);

(ii) 1, 2 & 3 = different uses of the word, e.g. as a noun – a fuss; as a verb – to fuss;

(iii) *n.* = noun;

(iv) = the meaning(s);

(v) *vb.* = verb;

(vi) example of usage (italic type);

(vii) foll. = followed;

(viii) *Brit.* = British;

(ix) *adj.* = adjective;

(x) *adv.* = adverb.

6 By using this key, what can we find out about 'fuss'? Make a list of four points, and remember to use your A4 sheet

We can find out:

- that it can be used as a noun or as a verb or (with other letters added) as an adjective;
- what it means;
- words and phrases that we can form from it (e.g. 'fusspot', 'made a fuss');
- that the compilers of the dictionary are not sure how the word came to be formed, what its *origin* was;
- how to spell it.

We can sum up by saying that the dictionary entry gives help in establishing the word's

- meaning and uses;
- spelling;
- origin.

I have missed out one other important kind of information the dictionary can give – pronunciation. Details of how to pronounce a word are given here in brackets after the first word of each entry. You'll notice that the word in brackets is made up of a combination of normal letters and strange symbols, for example 'fʌs' after fuss. To understand the meaning of these letters we need to refer to the 'pronunciation key' at the beginning of the dictionary. This key lists the symbols and their meaning. So we can find out that 'ʌ' has the same sound as 'u' in the word 'cut (kʌt)'.

What kind of word?

Immediately after each entry, the dictionary tells us how that word is used in the language. Some common abbreviations here are:

a. (or adj.)	=	adjective
adv.	=	adverb
n.	=	noun
vb.	=	verb
prep.	=	preposition
conj.	=	conjunction

Here are some examples:

jacaranda	n.
flippant	a.
dragnet	n.

You may not be very sure what these 'parts of speech' mean, but I don't want you to worry about this, for the following reasons:

- The description of language used by the dictionary is, many would think, an outdated one. It can be unnecessary and misleading.
- You don't need to be able to describe the language to use it properly. We all learn to speak our language from early childhood onwards, and we don't necessarily need to label the various words we use. We use them correctly, quite naturally – e.g. we don't say 'It's a sunnily morning' or 'He ran the road up' or 'Road up the he ran'.

Just to prove this for yourself, rewrite the following sentences so that they make sense.

a I tea want of cup a.

b Lovely a day it is.

c Aches tummy my.

a I want a cup of tea.

b It is a lovely day.

c My tummy aches.

You didn't need your dictionary to do this: you used your common sense.

We do still, though, need to understand the dictionary's abbreviations on occasions. Some words, for example, have more than one use. Look at 'fuss'. It can be used as a noun or as a verb. Even if you don't understand the terms 'noun' and 'verb', you can still understand the two different uses by looking at the other clues the dictionary gives. These may come in the form of phrases that include the word used as a noun or as a verb.

The *sense* of the phrases will show you how the word is being used in each case.

By using the context and by looking at your dictionary, answer the following SAQ.

'Object' has two main uses – as a verb and as a noun. In the following sentence it is used once in each way. Say when it is being used as a noun and when as a verb.

It was a hideous object and she did not object when her daughter took it to a local jumble sale.

The first use is as a noun, the second a verb. Note that verbs have distinctive endings '-s' (she object*s*); '-ing' (she is object*ing*); '-ed' (she object*ed*).

So if you're stuck over a word, and you don't know whether it is being used as a noun, verb, or adjective, try substituting the various dictionary meanings for it, and use your common sense.

If you're interested in the description of language, and want to learn more about it, see *Self-Access Grammar* by Erica Buckmaster, published by the National Extension College, 1990.

Adding to a word

Some words are the same in their noun form as in their verb form. A typical example is fuss – *a* fuss, *to* fuss. Other words can easily be changed, by adding a letter or letters, into a different kind of word (e.g. fuss-*y* turns the word into an adjective – 'a *fussy* person').

Abbreviations

Your dictionary – whatever its title and publisher – will have a list of abbreviations and symbols. You can't hope to remember all these, and there's no reason why you should try. Many of them refer to the *origins* of words in other languages:

L	=	Latin
G	=	Greek

Try to learn the more important ones, though. We've looked at some of these already. Here are some others you may come across and should be able to learn:

abbr.	=	abbreviation;
colloq.	=	colloquial;
dial.	=	dialect;
esp.	=	especially;
orig.	=	origin, originally;
sl.	=	slang.

When you come across abbreviations you don't know, always look them up. The more use you make of your dictionary the more abbreviations you'll be able to remember!

UNIT 4 USING THE DICTIONARY TO FIND MEANING

What this unit is about

By the time you have finished your work in this unit, you should be able to:

- ➜ use your dictionary as one way of working out what a word means;
- ➜ use your dictionary to find synonyms for words;
- ➜ use your dictionary to find the meanings of prefixes and suffixes;
- ➜ say why dictionary meanings are not, and can never be, any more than guides.

Introduction

First look at these examples of what happens when you don't look up meanings.

> *This is a particularly serious offence which we have to deal with severely, as a detergent to anyone in the same mind.* (Leicester Mercury)

> *The judge will have the power to order off any dog that commits a fragrant error.* (Gowerton & District Annual Show Schedule)

1 Write out the word that is being misused in each sentence. Can you suggest the word that should have been used?

detergent (should be deterrent)

fragrant (should be flagrant)

Actually, these are probably printing errors (one letter is wrong in each case) and you might look out for others in your local paper or in any magazines you buy.

But sometimes we confuse the meanings of two words that look and sound much the same. Here's an example from an essay I've just been marking:

> *He contributed the success of the team to the brilliance of the captain's batting.*

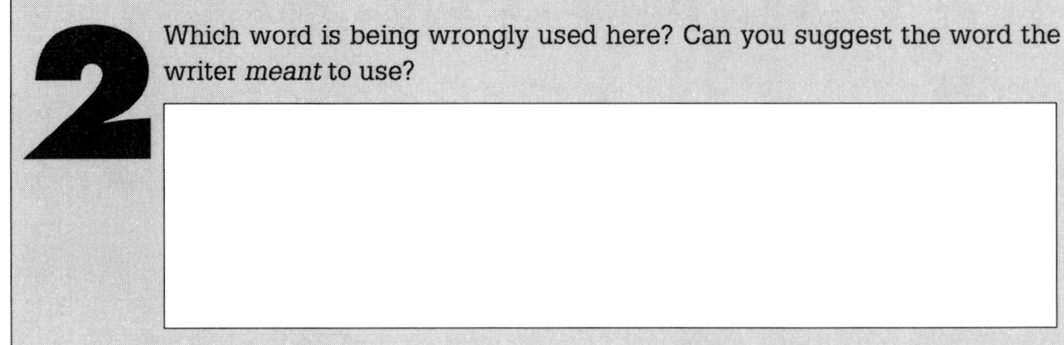

Which word is being wrongly used here? Can you suggest the word the writer *meant* to use?

Contributed should read *attributed*. Check both words in your dictionary.

The writer could have said, in other words:

> *He claimed that the success of the team was a result of the brilliance of the captain's batting.*

We can quite easily make such mistakes. In this unit I aim to show how a dictionary can help you avoid making them.

Finding the meaning of words

At the beginning of this unit under 'What this unit is about' there is a list of four statements. These are our objectives in this unit.

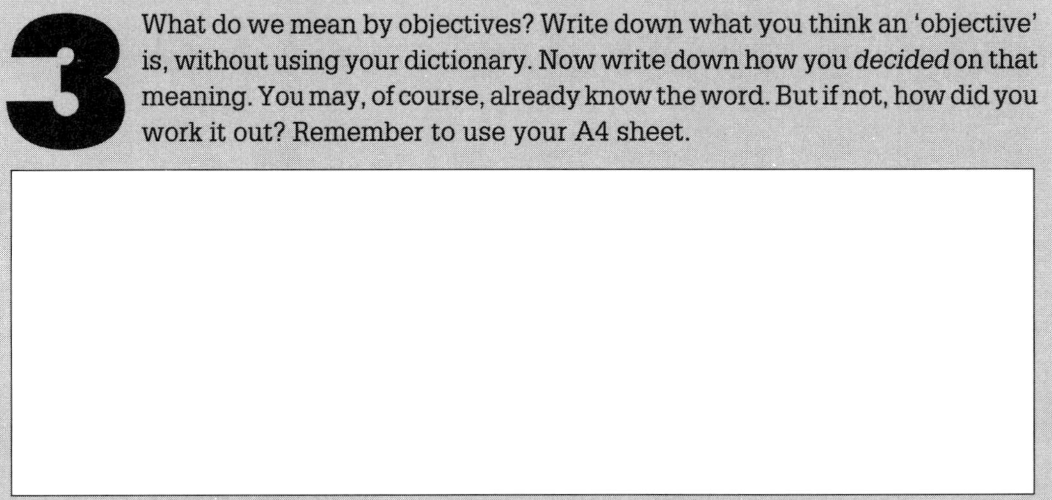

What do we mean by objectives? Write down what you think an 'objective' is, without using your dictionary. Now write down how you *decided* on that meaning. You may, of course, already know the word. But if not, how did you work it out? Remember to use your A4 sheet.

Presumably you looked at the passage, read it through carefully, and in particular looked at the sixteen introductory words. These tell you quite clearly that we want you to learn certain things, and to reach certain standards. So an objective is something we are *aiming at*. Did you manage to work out some such meaning, just by using your common sense? (Look back to Unit 3 where we pointed out how far you can get by using common sense and considering the *context* of a word.)

Now turn to your dictionary, and look up the word 'objective'.

You probably found this quite confusing, as in most dictionaries many different meanings are given. Unless you had a good idea of the *kind* of meaning you were looking for, and had understood the passage, you might well have been lost even if you had used your dictionary.

Here is the entry for 'objective' given in the *Collins New Compact:*

> **objective** (əbˈdʒɛktɪv) *adj.* **1.** having existence independent of the mind; real. **2.** undistorted by personal feelings or bias: *an objective opinion.* **3.** of or relating to actual facts as opposed to thoughts or feelings: *objective evidence.* **4.** *Grammar.* denoting a case of nouns and pronouns, that identifies the direct object of a verb or preposition. ~*n.* **5.** a goal; aim. **6.** an actual fact; reality. **7.** *Grammar.* the objective case. **8.** *Optics.* the lens nearest to the object observed in an optical instrument. —**objectival** (ˌɒbdʒɛkˈtaɪvəl) *adj.* —**obˈjectively** *adv.* —**ˌobjecˈtivity** *n.*

When we used the word 'objective' above, we were using it as a noun – 'the' or 'an' objective – rather than as a verb or an adjective. To spot the use helps you to move quickly to the correct place in the dictionary entry. You'd skip the first four meanings given ('objective' as an adjective) and move to the *noun* (*n.*) use.

Sometimes the dictionary can be more directly helpful in establishing a meaning. You may be reading a passage that contains words you've not met before – for example a car repair manual, a do-it-yourself book or a handicrafts magazine.

Read the following passage from a popular medical encyclopaedia and underline any words whose meanings you're not sure of.

> *diaphragm* Sheet of muscle separating the thorax from the abdomen. Its fibres arise from the lumbar vertebrae, the lower ribs, and the lower end of the sternum. They converge on a flat sheet of dense fibrous tissue, the central tendon. The whole structure forms a sort of dome.

(From *The Penguin Medical Encyclopaedia,*
P. Wingate, 2nd Edition 1976)

Take your list of words and look them up in your dictionary. Does your dictionary help you to understand the passage?

You should have found all the words you needed. If the passage had been more technical (e.g. written for doctors or nurses) you wouldn't have found the dictionary of much help. Look at this extract from a medical journal:

> Concurrent admin. of coumarin-type anticoagulants or heparin. Simultaneous admin. of aspirin reduces fenoprofen absorption. (*MIMS*, vol. 18, No. 1, Jan. 1976)

You'd need a medical dictionary (and a lot of experience) to make much sense of writing like this!

So your dictionary can give you help in looking up the meanings of most words in daily use. When it also gives you a phrase in which the word is used (e.g. *fulsome – fulsome compliments*), you are helped even more, as we saw in the previous unit. Small general dictionaries cannot give you much help of this kind. You'd need to consult a larger dictionary for more examples of the words used in phrases and sentences.

Here is one more example of using the dictionary to check on the meanings of words.

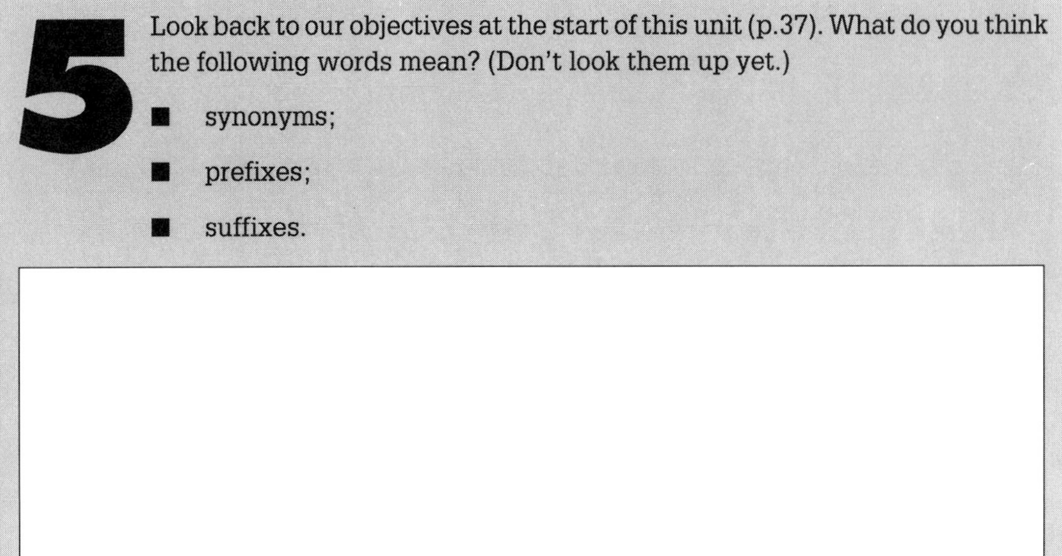

5 Look back to our objectives at the start of this unit (p.37). What do you think the following words mean? (Don't look them up yet.)

- synonyms;
- prefixes;
- suffixes.

Now check your meanings against those given in the dictionary.

You should have found this fairly straightforward. The entries in most dictionaries are quite brief, and specific: there aren't many alternative meanings to choose from.

Words used in special ways

We've been looking at words which we might not understand. Our problem with these words is a simple one:

- we don't know what they mean;
- so we have to look them up;
- then we check on various meanings given until one seems to fit.

But sometimes we come across words whose meanings we *think* we understand. But in fact we may be deceiving ourselves. The words *may* be used in a special sense.

Good examples come from sport. Imagine someone who knew English but had never seen or heard of the game of cricket. He or she would be puzzled to hear or read sentences like:

He bowled a maiden over.

He was standing at silly mid on but moved to long leg at the end of the over.

He was fielding at silly point.

In themselves, each of these words is quite simple ('maiden', 'over', 'silly', 'mid', 'on' etc.). But they are being used in a special sense.

6 Choose a sport, hobby, or activity you are interested in, or your job. Write down as many words of this kind, used in connection with your subject, as you can think of.

(continued opposite)

If you are an expert in any activity you will, of course, know the special meanings of these words.

I can't know what you are expert in, but I'm going to choose for my main example a cookery recipe. I have tried many times to follow recipes but have been disappointed, partly because I didn't fully understand the special ways in which simple words are used.

Look at this extract from a recipe, taken from the side of a sugar packet. It's for a Victoria sandwich cake.

> Cream butter and sugar together. Gradually add the eggs, beating thoroughly. Fold in the flour. Put into two greased 6 inch sandwich tins. Bake in a moderate oven (375°F. mark 5, 190°C.) for 15–20 minutes. Sandwich together with jam or butter cream when cool. Dredge with sugar and serve.

You may already know the cookery meanings of all these words. But even if you do, I'd like you to pretend that you are someone who has never cooked a meal in their life.

7 Underline or write out some words in the passage that such a person would need to beware of, since they are being used in a special *cookery* sense. Use your A4 sheet to cover up my response.

I underlined:

- cream;
- beating;
- fold in;
- sandwich tin;
- bake;
- sandwich;
- butter cream;
- dredge.

These are all words familiar to us in daily life, but with special meanings in cookery. There is a whole host of others, of course, not in the passage – e.g. whip, blend, whisk, mix, stir. You need to be aware of the meanings – e.g. when you *whisk* you put air into a mixture; when you *fold in* you keep air out. Look at the following extract from a recipe for egg sponge:

1 Whisk eggs and sugar together.

2 Fold in flour.

What would happen if you folded the eggs into the sugar and whisked in the flour?

Disaster. Or perhaps, nothing!

Now turn back to the words you listed from the recipe for Victoria sandwich cake. Here is the *Collins New Compact* entry for 'cream'.

cream (kriːm) *n.* **1.** the fatty part of milk, which rises to the top. **2.** anything, such as a cosmetic, resembling cream in consistency. **3.** the best part of something; pick. **4.** any of various foods resembling or containing cream. ~*adj.* **5.** yellowish-white. ~*vb.* **6.** to remove the cream from (milk). **7.** to beat (foodstuffs) to a light creamy consistency. **8.** (sometimes foll. by *off*) to take away the best part of. **9.** to prepare or cook (foodstuffs) with cream or milk. [Late Latin *crāmum*] —'**creamy** *adj.*

'Cream' is being used here as a verb (see use 6 of *cream* under the dictionary entry). Four uses of the word as a verb are given.

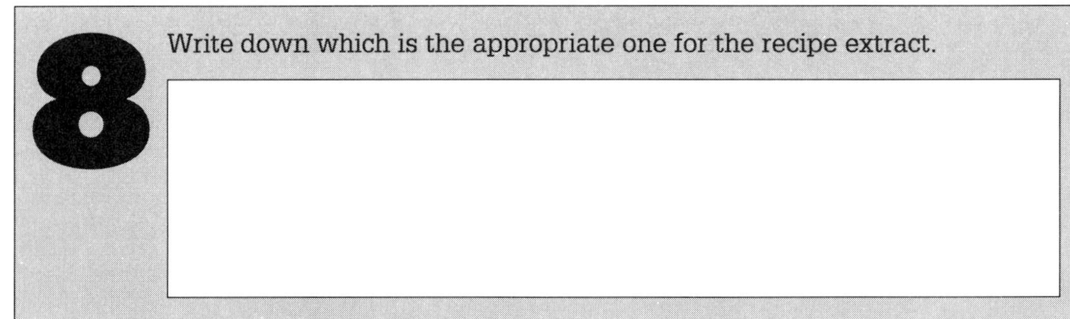
8 Write down which is the appropriate one for the recipe extract.

To beat (foodstuffs) to a light creamy consistency.

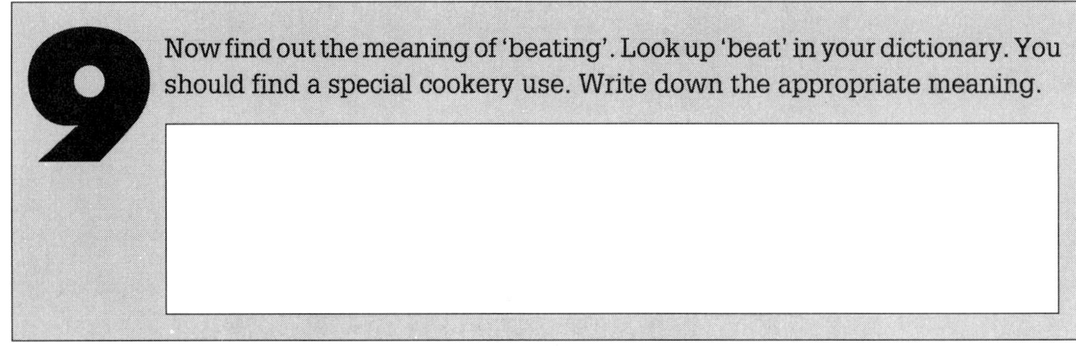
9 Now find out the meaning of 'beating'. Look up 'beat' in your dictionary. You should find a special cookery use. Write down the appropriate meaning.

My dictionary has 'stir or whisk vigorously'.

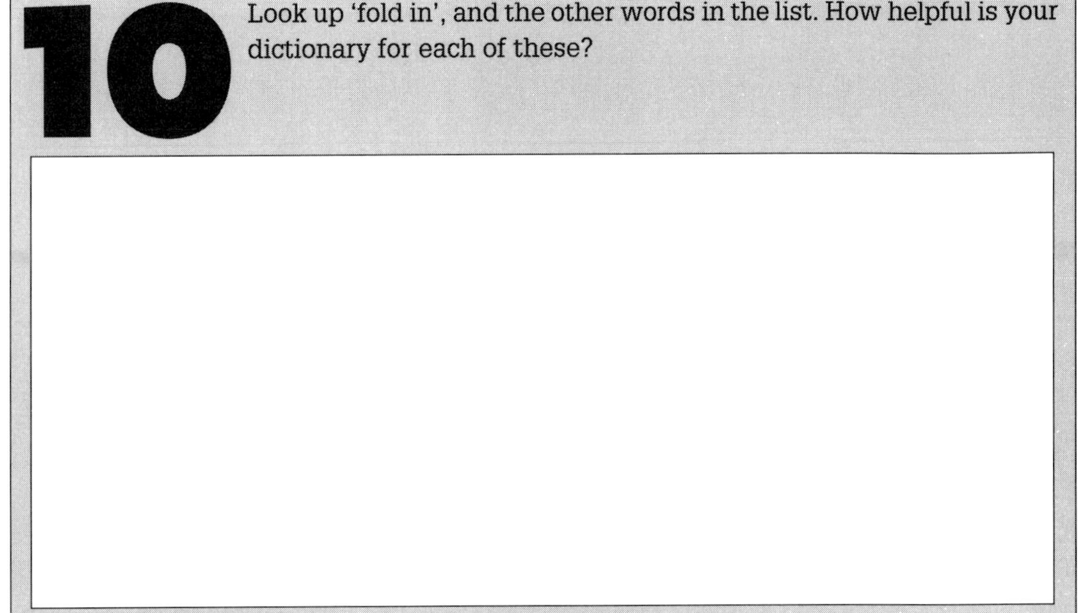

Look up 'fold in', and the other words in the list. How helpful is your dictionary for each of these?

My dictionary is very helpful on 'fold in' and 'bake'. 'Sandwich tin' isn't defined, and neither is 'butter cream'. 'Dredge' is clearly defined in its cookery use. This was quite a new meaning of the word for me.

So in our recipe we have been able to use the dictionary quite extensively, though notice that it cannot cover everything, and that it cannot show us how to carry out the activities it defines. We have also been looking at the English language at work and have been standing back from it, growing more conscious of it.

The more we know about cookery, and the more cooking we have carried out, the better we are at understanding what its special language involves. This applies whatever subject we are dealing with.

Sailing, physics, chess, insurance – all have their own special vocabularies, and the deeper we go into such subjects the easier they become. This is why it helps to make a booklet of new words in your subject area: to understand the language used is to understand the ideas and theories. So if you are taking other courses alongside this book, buy a small notebook and divide it up, A to Z. As you come across special words for your subject (e.g. 'force' in physics, 'determine' and 'correlation' in social science) enter these on the appropriate page of the notebook, along with definitions of their meanings.

Now try some more SAQs on using your dictionary to establish meaning.

Here is an entry from an insurance policy. Read it, and answer the question below.

Taxation

By Inland Revenue concession, benefits are free of tax for one complete fiscal year and taxable thereafter as unearned income.

Look up 'concession' and 'fiscal', and any other words you need, and then rewrite this statement so that it would make sense to a non-expert. Remember to use your A4 sheet.

(continued overleaf)

Taxation

The Inland Revenue has agreed (*concession*) that money gained (under this policy) is free of tax for one tax year (the public revenue year). From then on (*thereafter*) it will be taxed under the same terms as those in operation for unearned income.

Here is an extract from *Jude the Obscure* by Thomas Hardy.

> He began to see that the town life was a book of humanity infinitely more palpitating, varied, and compendious than the gown life.

This means, roughly, that the life of the town (i.e. the non-university life) was much better than the life of the university colleges in Oxford ('gown life'). But Hardy doesn't just say 'better', or 'fuller'. Like all great novelists, he chooses his words carefully.

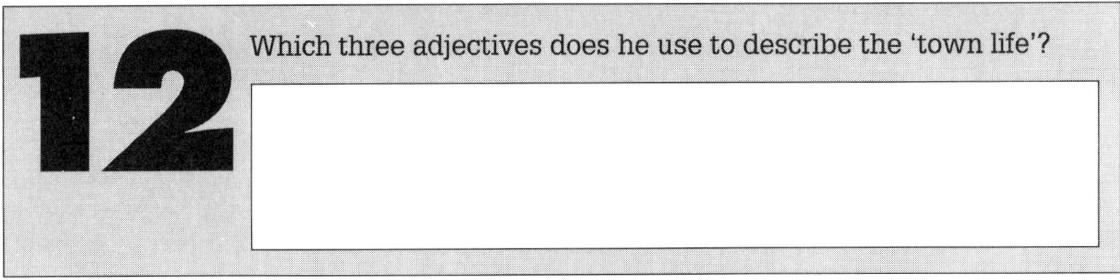

'Palpitating', 'varied' and 'compendious'.

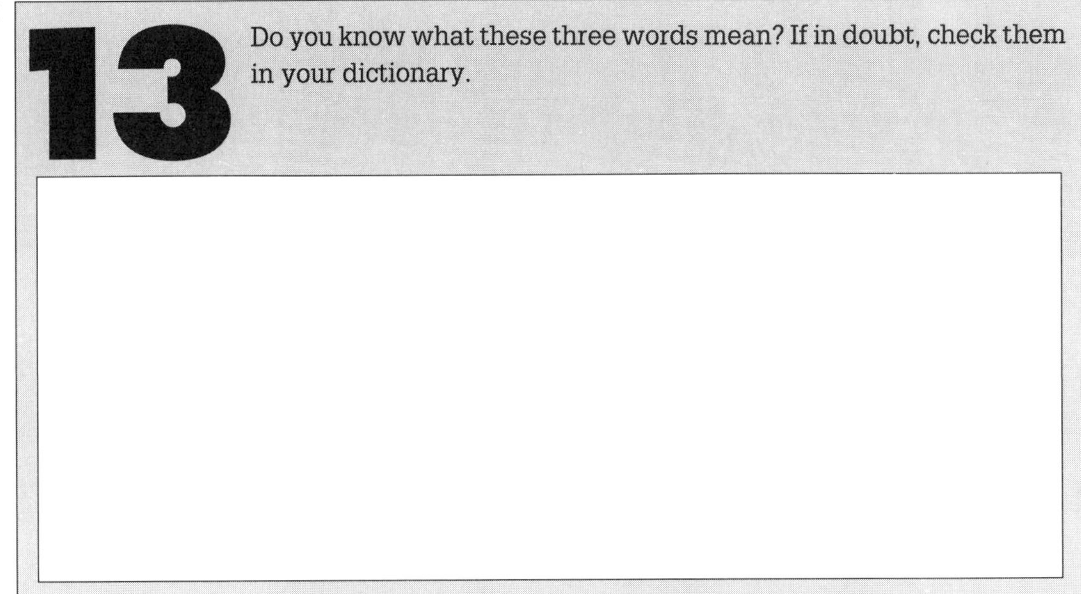

- palpitating = trembling or throbbing (note that palpitat*ing* isn't actually given in my dictionary, but it's easy enough to form this word from 'palpitate'. *-ing* is a suffix, as we'll see later)
- varied = diverse
- compendious = brief but comprehensive

So the three words are carefully chosen to describe the life exactly. We need to be aware of the differences in the meanings of the words, and the dictionary can help us in this.

Here's another extract from a novel – *Ulysses* by James Joyce. Mr Leopold Bloom is preparing breakfast:

> On the boil sure enough: a plume of steam from the spout. He scalded and rinsed out the teapot and put in four full spoons of tea, tilting the kettle then to let water flow in. Having set it to draw, he took off the kettle and crushed the pan flat on the live coals and watched the lump of butter slide and melt. While he unwrapped the kidney the cat mewed hungrily against him. Give her too much meat she won't mouse. Say they won't eat pork. Kosher. Here. He let the bloodsmeared paper fall to her and dropped the kidney amid the sizzling butter sauce. Pepper. He sprinkled it through his fingers, ringwise, from the chipped eggcup.

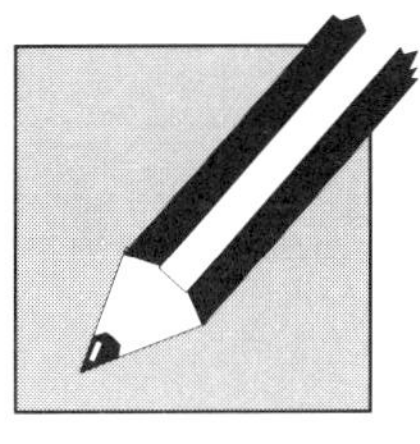

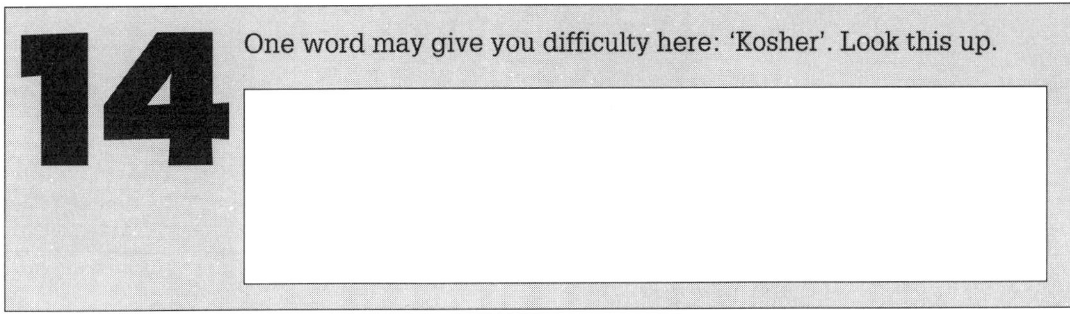

14 One word may give you difficulty here: 'Kosher'. Look this up.

But your dictionary has its limits, as was pointed out in Unit 2 of this book. For example, you won't find it much help in dealing with this passage from *An Introduction to Human Development* by K. Lovell:

> In Chapter 1 it was pointed out that when the genotypic and phenotypic sex is inconsistent, most persons think of themselves as belonging to the sex which they represent or approach phenotypically.

Or this very different passage from *Ulysses*. Stephen is walking along the beach:

> Five, six: the *nacheinander*. Exactly: and that is the ineluctable modality of the audible. Open your eyes. No. Jesus! If I fell through the *nebeneinander* ineluctably. I am getting on nicely in the dark. My ash sword hangs at my side. Tap with it: they do. My two feet in his boots are at the end of his legs, *nebeinander*. Sounds solid: made by the mallet of *Los Demiurgos*.

The first passage is difficult because it uses the specialist terms of social science (genotypic, phenotypic). You'd need a more detailed dictionary than the *Collins New Compact* to work out the meanings of these terms (e.g. a dictionary of psychology).

The second is difficult in a different way. It gives a character's thought processes, and the character knows a lot of philosophy. We'd have to work hard to find out what the philosophical terms he uses mean, and they won't be found in any ordinary dictionary. Just to look up the odd word isn't much use, anyway, as what we need to possess is some sort of philosophical frame of reference.

15

Finally, have a go at writing your own 'meanings' of everyday words. Then compare your efforts with the dictionary definitions. Try doing this for:

- sleeve;
- cup;
- egg.

This SAQ should help you understand what it feels like to be the compiler of a dictionary.

Synonyms

Earlier in this unit you looked up 'synonym' in the dictionary.

16

Check back

- to what this word means;
- to the second objective given at the start of this unit.

When might you need to find a synonym?

When you are writing, have used a certain word once and don't want to repeat it, e.g.

> *The building was florid. The windows were decorated in a florid style with florid motifs.*

This is dull and unspecific. Using your dictionary, it could be rewritten like this:

> *The building was florid. The windows were decorated in a showy style, with ornate motifs.*

To look up a word can (as we saw with the example from Thomas Hardy) give you a series of more precise meanings. Thus:

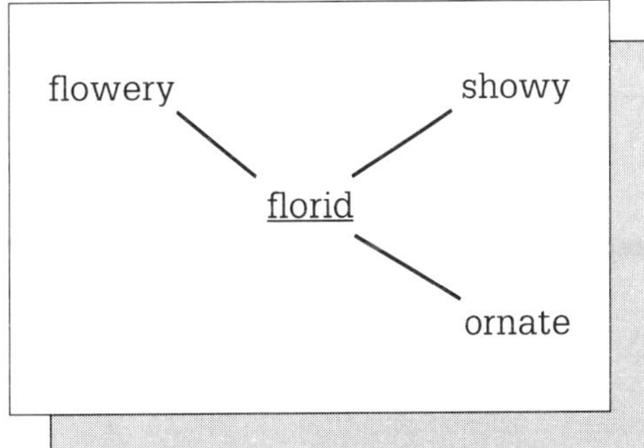

17

Use your dictionary to find synonyms for the words underlined in the following passages. Try to find words which:

- vary the language and stop it becoming repetitive;
- convey the meaning more exactly.

(Use your dictionary for this, even if you can suggest words without its help. We want to see how good the dictionary is for this purpose.)

a *The sea shore was shining. The tide was going out, leaving an expanse of* <u>*shining*</u> *sand. Small pools* <u>*shone*</u> *in the evening light.* <u>*Small*</u> *creatures scuttled along the sands.*

b *The power of the unions must be* <u>*cut.*</u> *They have* <u>*cut down*</u> *the rights of ordinary individuals in our society. They have* <u>*cut*</u> *choice and* <u>*cut*</u> *the standard of living of the self-employed.*

Just by using a short general dictionary it is possible to find synonyms to make these passages both more interesting and more exact. Here are examples of how the passages could be altered:

a The sea shore was shining. The tide was going out, leaving an expanse of gleaming sand. Small pools reflected in the evening light. Little creatures scuttled along the sands.

(Though it's important to notice the limitations of the dictionary, you may have done better without it! I was surprised, for example, not to find 'shimmer' mentioned under 'shine' in my dictionary, and I'd expect to find 'tiny' under 'small'.)

b The power of the unions must be pruned. They have reduced the rights of ordinary individuals in our society. They have limited choice and brought down the standard of living of the self-employed.

(You probably had to hunt around the entry on *cut* to find alternatives and, as always, to adapt and to use your own common sense. You could also keep at least one of the four 'cuts' in the original.)

Thus the dictionary can help you to find synonyms. There is, though, another reference book which will give you more help, and that is *The Thesaurus of English Words and Phrases* by Roget (often just called *Roget's Thesaurus*). You'll find this in any reference library, and it is also available in paperback.

Prefixes and suffixes

Again, look back to your definitions of these words (p.40), and at our third objective for this unit (p.37).

A prefix is, put simply, a bit stuck on at the front of a word.

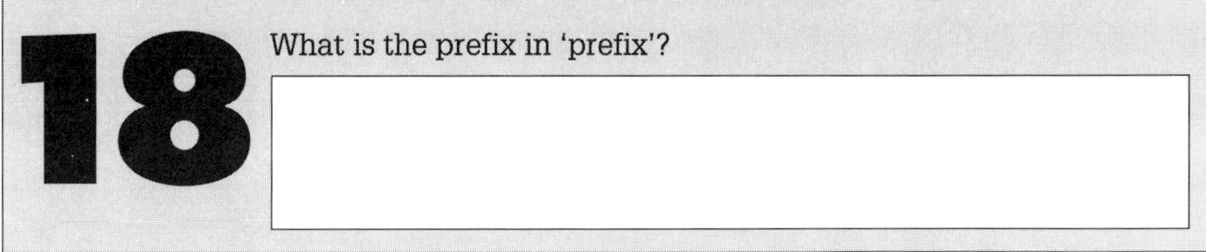

'pre ...'. It's the bit placed before 'fix'.

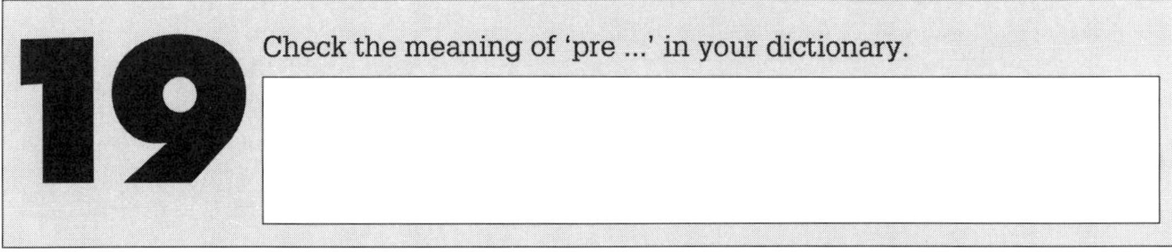

'before'. Thus prefix means 'fixed before'.

Notice all the other examples of words beginning with 'pre ...' in your dictionary. Can you see how, in the majority of cases, the meaning 'before' is included?

A *suffix* is similar, except that in this case the letters are added at the *end* of a word. Examples of suffixes are:

- ive;
- ible;
- ing.

(Do you remember our earlier example? *Palpitate* becomes *palpitating* by the addition of the suffix '...ing'.)

These two units of language, the prefix and suffix, are very important and it helps to recognise them, as you can then begin to break down the meaning of words.

20

Take the prefix *trans*. What does this mean?

How does this help you to understand the meanings of:

- transfer;
- transfigure;
- translucent;
- transport?

Make up your own definitions for each of these, and *then* check each word in the dictionary.

'Trans' means across, beyond, crossing, through. So:

- transfer: to cause to *cross* from one point to another;
- transfigure: to go *beyond* the human to the supernatural;
- translucent: letting light *through*;
- transport: to carry someone or something from one place *across* to another.

My definitions probably aren't identical to those given in your dictionary, but I've tried to show how an understanding of what *trans* means can help you to break up a word and tackle it in its smaller parts. Look through more of the *trans* words in your dictionary and see how the meaning of the prefix is basically there in each example.

21

Another very important prefix is *un*- (meaning *not*). List ten words having this prefix (e.g. unbend, unlock) without looking at your dictionary. Then look for an entry under *un*.

You could have listed any of a large number of words beginning *un-*. The *Collins New Compact* gives over 220 full entries.

Here is one of its entries under *un*:

un-[2] *prefix forming verbs.* **1.** denoting reversal of an action or state: *uncover; untie.* **2.** denoting removal from, release, or deprivation: *unharness; unthrone.* **3.** (intensifier): *unloose.* [Old English *un-, on-*]

22 Go back to the three suffixes quoted earlier:

- ive;
- ible;
- ing.

Write down at least one word which finishes in each of these groups of letters. Then check your word in the dictionary; e.g. write down 'digestive', and then look it up.

In this section I have introduced you to the prefix and the suffix, and at the same time tried to show you how useful they are in breaking a word down into manageable parts. You can learn how the language works by doing this.

23 Finally, look back to our last objective for this unit (p.37). Look quickly through the whole unit and write down as many points as you can to show why the dictionary cannot be the only, or the perfect, source of advice about a word's meaning.

You may have noted some or all of the following points:

1. Sometimes the dictionary gives several different meanings, and you have to test each one in turn, or have some idea beforehand, for the dictionary to be of any help (as in our example of 'objective').

2. Not all words can be included, e.g. 'sandwich' is in, and 'tin' is in, but not 'sandwich tin' (and not 'butter cream'). The dictionary cannot include every word. We still have to use our common sense, and *think*! (Unit 2 had things to say on this, too.)

3. Some passages are difficult to understand. This is only partly because of individual words; it's more that the ideas are so complex that it's a matter of coming to terms with these. (Remember the extracts from *Human Development* and from *Ulysses*?)

4. We always have to work out what an individual word means *in its context*. This is particularly true of:

   - words with several meanings;
   - words which have specialist, as well as ordinary, meanings.

5. A further complication is that words change their meanings over a period of time. We will look at this in some detail in Unit 7.

UNIT 5 USING THE DICTIONARY TO FIND SPELLING

What this unit is about

This unit aims to help you in a number of ways. Part 1 is meant only for some of you. It is for people who worry about their spelling.

By the time you have worked through Part 1, you should be able to:

- ➜ understand the nature of the problem of spelling;
- ➜ plan how you can begin to improve your spelling;
- ➜ find a technique (or techniques) that is particularly suitable for your spelling.

People who do need this part of the unit will also need to study Part 2, but good spellers may well prefer to move straight on to Part 2.

By the time you have finished your work on Part 2, you should be able to:

- ➜ find words in the dictionary, even when you have little idea how to spell them;
- ➜ make certain that you choose the right spelling where words that sound the same are spelt differently;
- ➜ find out the spelling of words which do not appear in the dictionary as separate entries;
- ➜ find out the correct spelling when you change (or *inflect*) words (for example, when you use plurals or the past tense of a verb).

Part 1: Improving your spelling

Children learn to talk long before they learn to write and read. Although we have been writing for only about four thousand years, we have been talking far longer. This leads some theorists to claim that skill with language is built into our genes. When missionaries penetrated central Africa in the late nineteenth century they found hundreds of languages, none of them with written forms. The people they found were articulate and intelligent.

These facts seem irrelevant to spelling problems, but they aren't. Most of us think that spelling is a basic part of our knowledge of words, but this is quite wrong. We can know almost all there is to know about what words mean, and about how to use them, even if we have never heard of the idea of writing. Take, for example, the word 'peculiar'. Now if someone asked me what that word means, or how he or she should use it, I can be very helpful. I understand the word very well. But when that person asks me, 'How do you spell it?' I am stuck.

Everyone has some difficulties in spelling – we all have words that we always get wrong – 'bogey words'. To improve spelling requires a number of things. You must aim to:

- get into the habit of finding out spellings;
- be prepared to make a written-out list and to learn the spellings that always cause you trouble;
- be prepared to guess spellings, but always check them in your dictionary.

Don't leave a word alone if you're unsure about it: check it. And do ask other people – don't be shy about it, they will be keen to help. But again, check the word later.

A spelling strategy

Making a list

You must start a list of the words you can't spell. Begin your list just after you have written an essay or letter.

Read over what you have been writing, and recall the words that gave you trouble or worried you. Look up their spelling and put them on a list.

Now I suggest that you buy yourself a compact exercise book. Divide it into alphabetical sections: A, B, C, etc. Leave extra space for common letters. Now enter under the relevant letter the correct spellings of words that bother you. I wouldn't try for alphabetical order within each letter section.

In your next few pieces of writing watch carefully for words that you aren't confident of spelling. As they come up, check them in the dictionary and put them on your list, unless they already appear. Soon, you will have a list of words that you can't spell confidently. It won't be complete, but that doesn't matter just now.

Analysing your list

As soon as you have made a list you should look at it carefully. Is there a pattern to your problem? It is not always easy to analyse spelling errors, but it is well worth trying. For some people it can make the improvement of their spelling very much easier.

Perhaps your list is full, not of words which you can't spell, but of little modifications that we make to words when we use them. For example, you may be able to spell 'know', but not 'knew'. You may have trouble with the past tense of verbs, or with plurals, or with something else like this. If you suspect that this is the case, look at the sections on inflexion later in this unit. These, with any general section on inflexion given in the introduction to your dictionary, will help you a lot.

Perhaps you can't spell the ends of words. It might be worth your while to look over and even to learn the list of suffixes given at the start of some dictionaries. Not everyone, I must stress, will feel that learning suffixes will help them. If you are one of these, don't learn this list.

If you can identify one particular problem as the source of your difficulties, you will be conscious of what to watch in your spelling. This will be one major gain. You will also know when to reach for your dictionary and, by paying special attention to your weakness, you will find that you set your mind to work on it. You may also hit on short cuts to speed up your improvement. If you aren't able to identify specific problems, you won't be able to use short cuts – but you can certainly cure your poor spelling.

Learning spellings

There are many different ways of learning spellings and the secret is to find the one or ones that suit you. Here are some possibilities; I suggest that you try out each one in turn and use the one you feel most confident about.

Look, cover, write, check

Look at a word, copy it. As soon as you feel confident, try covering the original before you write it down. Check it if you get stuck, look at the word again, and cover it again – until you start getting it right.

Syllables

One way of learning longer words is to break them up into syllables. For example, 'transcontinental' can be broken up into 'trans - con - tin - en - tal' or 'yesterday' into 'yes - ter - day'. This can make it easier to remember the correct spelling, because the words become more manageable.

The sound of words

Similarly, it can sometimes help to pronounce a word as it is spelt – as, for example, in 'Wed - nes - day', 'se - par - ate', 'ba - na - na'.

Rules

Some spelling rules can also help, for example words ending in 'y' change the 'y' to 'i' when they add a suffix (for example: 'happy – happiness', 'beauty – beautiful').

(See Part 2 of this unit for some other rules on inflexion.)

Mnemonics

Look this word up in your dictionary. There are ways of remembering spelling by tricks, rhymes etc. – for example '*eleph*ant's t*eleph*one', 'fi*sh*' and '*ch*ips' for 'sh' and 'ch'.

You should by now have tried some of these methods. Whichever one or ones you choose, you will have to go back to the words several times if you want to learn them permanently.

Now study Part 2, for you will need to use your dictionary often, not only at first, but also as your spelling improves. A good speller is ready to use a dictionary, and to go on using one.

Part 2: Finding out how to spell a word

Spelling strategies are for those of us who feel that our minds are not efficient enough at the task of spelling well. The rest of us are fairly good at spelling, or perhaps almost completely reliable. If you fall into the last category, you won't be using this unit anyway! I, for one, am some way from being a totally reliable speller.

We quite good spellers don't need a spelling strategy. But we do need, if we're honest, the skill to solve any spelling problem that may come up. The rest of this unit aims to provide this skill. It will, of course, be essential reading for those who want to undertake the spelling strategy described in Part 1, for the heart of that was looking up spellings in a dictionary.

Before we start to discuss the problems of checking spelling in a dictionary, do remember that spelling is not *absolutely* rigid. Some words can be spelled two ways, and if you look up such a word in your dictionary it will appear under both spellings. Thus you may also find 'inflection' under 'inflexion'. The *Collins New Compact*, for example, has 'color' as '*U.S.* same as **colour**.'

We all know that dictionaries list words in alphabetical order; that is, according to their spelling. And they don't just order words by their first letter. If the first letter is the same, words are ordered by their second letter, so that 'cap' comes before 'cup', and then by their third letter, and so on.

The problem this creates is obvious. Words are listed in an order that depends on their spelling. So how can you look up the spelling if you can't spell the word already? In practice, this problem isn't as bad as it seems. Most of the time, we look up spelling to check what we think is right. If you're doing this, you will have absolutely no problem unless your idea of how to spell the word is wrong!

But what do you do if your opinion, or your guess, does turn out to be wrong, and you don't find the word where you expected it? And what happens if you really aren't sure about the most likely spelling? Either way, you have the same problem. The word you want is somewhere in the dictionary, but you don't know where. How then do you find it?

Finding words

Six times out of ten finding a word is easy. Take an example, 'separate'. Now, if you are like me, you won't be entirely sure about what is the fourth letter. But everyone would guess that the first three must be 'sep'.

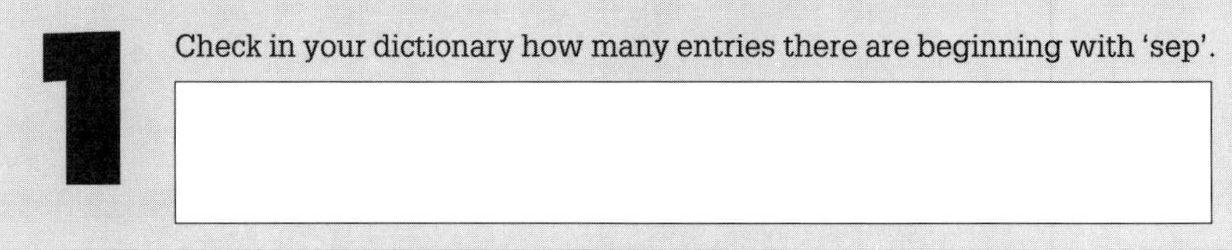

You see my point? 'Separate' isn't difficult to find.

This is because 'separate' is a word that starts out as it sounds. Now consider another word, 'banana'. Many people worry about the second letter of this. How would you check it? You could look right through the 'b' section, but I am sure you wouldn't.

The answer, of course, is that you would decide on the possibilities for the second letter, and check under each. You would probably try the most likely first. I might have guessed 'u' and 'a' in that order.

No doubt you have by now discovered one of the reasons why we recommend a pocket dictionary. It saves a lot of work when you are looking up a spelling. Looking up 'banana' in the *Oxford English Dictionary* would take some time!

The problem of finding a word is most difficult, of course, when you are unsure of even the first letter. This often happens with words beginning with 'k' and 'c', like 'keep' and 'creep'. There isn't any logic to help us choose between the opening letters in this case. The same problem can occur with 'c' and 's'. There is no apparent sense in the different openings of 'sender' and 'centre'.

What do *you* do if you are in doubt about these sorts of words? To take an example, how would you find out whether 'catamaran' begins with 'cat' or 'kat'? Think about it for a moment, and write your answer briefly.

(continued opposite)

I am sure you would do the sensible thing: decide the possible first letters, and look the word up under each. Probably you would look under the most likely letter first, and soon find the word.

Words you can't find

We all recognise this situation. You look up a word where you expect to find it. It isn't there. You think about other ways of spelling its first part. You look up these, but still you can't find the word. But it isn't a really rare word, so it must be in the dictionary. This is the dictionary-user's worst fear. What can you do?

Ask yourself two questions:

1 Is the word made up of parts that you *can* find?

4 As an example, find out from your dictionary what an 'endoskeleton', which insects possess, really is. Note down what you looked up.

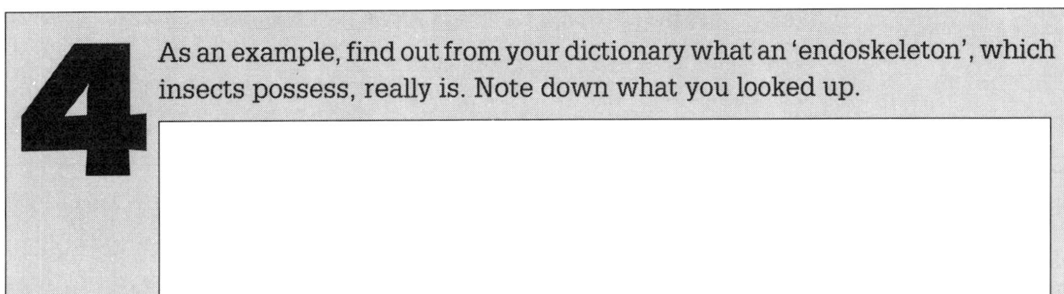

I hope you looked up 'endo' and 'skeleton'. You did work on prefixes like 'endo' in Unit 4.

2 Is the word listed under another word? Like 'beautiful', for example, which appears under 'beauty'.

If the answer to each of these questions is *no*, you have a real problem. How can you solve it, especially if there is no one around to ask?

There is only one solution that I know of. Try to think of a similar sounding word that you know is spelled oddly. This usually works beautifully. If you can't spell 'wrist', perhaps you know 'wrong'. There are other examples of this.

5 Write down some more common words that might give you a hint about where to look in your dictionary for 'knight' and 'psychology'.

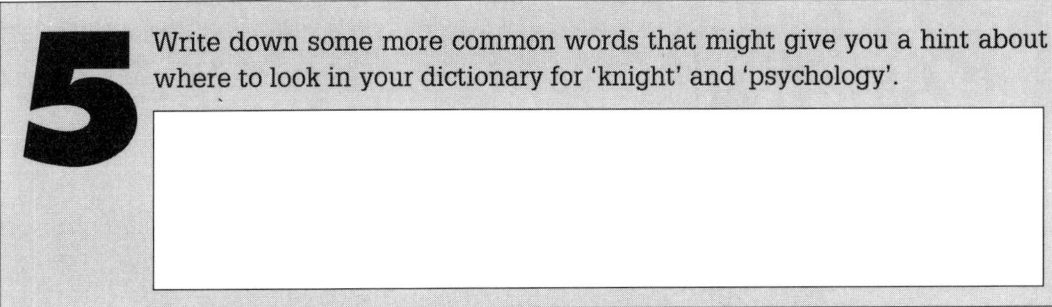

I can think of 'knife', 'knob', 'knickers', and, I hasten to add, 'psalm'.

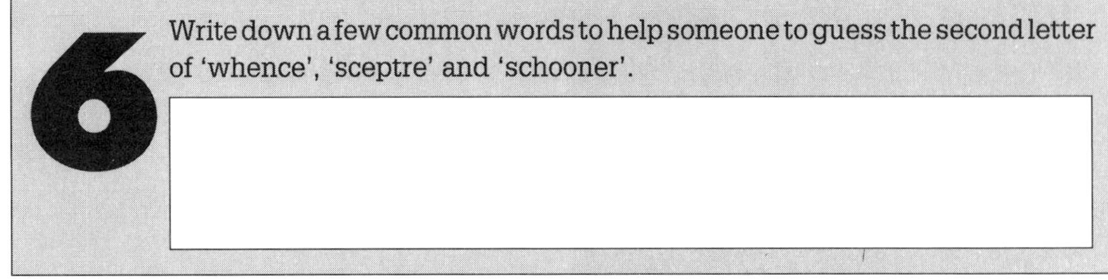

6 Write down a few common words to help someone to guess the second letter of 'whence', 'sceptre' and 'schooner'.

I'd suggest 'when', 'scene' and 'school'.

This is much the best way to solve the problem of odd spellings. If it doesn't work, you will have to find someone to ask. Always check the answer, and then enter the spelling in the margin of your dictionary where you first looked for it, to avoid future problems. I don't think that you will have to do this very often.

Avoiding mistakes

We have been studying words that are not spelled as you would expect. But you can meet a different problem in words that sound the same but are spelled differently.

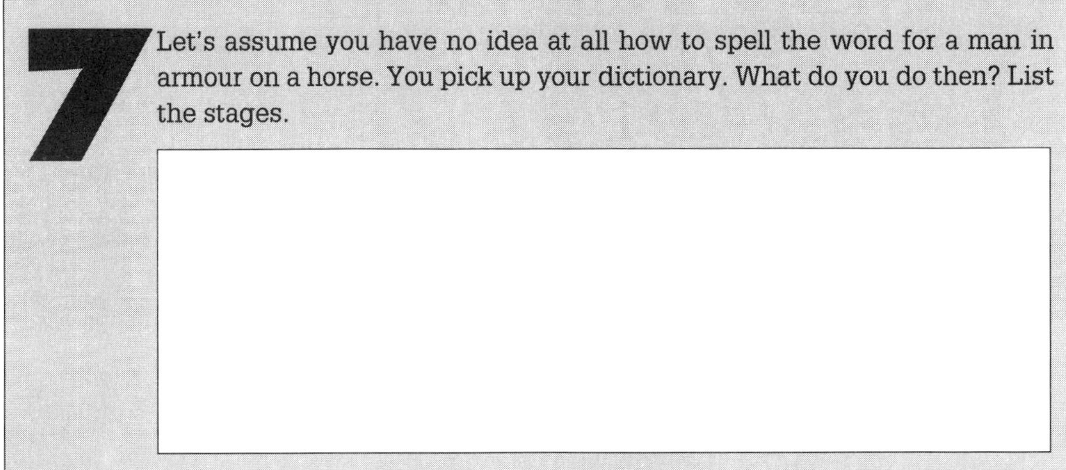

7 Let's assume you have no idea at all how to spell the word for a man in armour on a horse. You pick up your dictionary. What do you do then? List the stages.

This is what you might do.

1 You might think the word was spelled 'nite'. You would look this up and fail to find it.

2 You would think hard, and decide that the word must surely start with 'ni'.

3 You would go through the 'ni' section and find 'night'.

4 You would use this in your sentence. 'The night sat on the horse.'

Or would you? The second word is spelled wrongly.

8 Decide for yourself where the checking process went wrong, and why.

It went wrong, of course, after 3. But why? Surely because you failed to check the meaning that went with the spelling. It is always wise to glance at the meanings of words in the dictionary, or you may use one that means the wrong thing.

There are a number of quite separate words that sound alike, but are spelled differently.

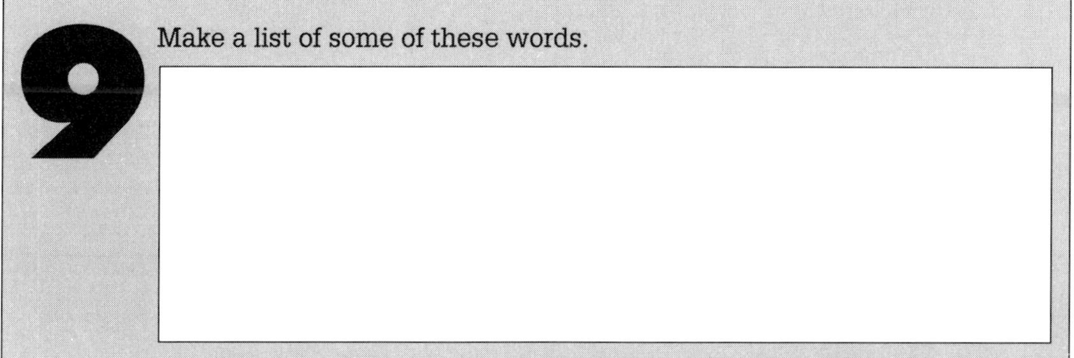

9 Make a list of some of these words.

The best known are 'which' and 'witch', 'their' and 'there' and 'to', 'two' and 'too'. If you don't bother to check the meaning that goes with the spelling of words like these, you will make mistakes.

'Missing' words

Sometimes you will not find a separate listing for the word you are looking for. This is because, to save space, words are lumped together. For example, 'swimming pool' may be listed under 'swim'. Sometimes there *is* a separate entry but one which refers you back to the main word. In the *Pocket Oxford*, for example, 'swollen' is listed and the entry reads 'see SWELL'. This is an example of a cross-reference, and it is put in to stop you getting lost.

Inflexion

The previous section was really about separate words that the dictionary lumps together to save space. But individual words change in little ways, depending on the rest of the sentence in which we use them. We change verbs in the past tense ('kiss' becomes 'kissed', for example). We change them if the action goes on ('kissing'). We change words when things belong to them ('the boy's dog') and when they are plural. And there are many more. These changes are small, and the dictionary calls them *inflexions*.

Everyone who reads this book knows how to change words when talking, but the dictionary does need to give us help in writing inflexions down. For you can hit real problems here. Do you double the last letter of the verb 'to fit' in the past tense? Do you change the final 'y' to an 'i' in the past tense of 'cry'?

Some dictionaries have a section on inflexion. On the next page, for example, is the relevant part of the *Collins New Compact*.

This extract gives you rules which tell you how to write down the inflected forms of 'regular' – that is orthodox – words. If a word doesn't follow these rules – if it is 'irregular' – this information is included in the individual entry.

Using the 'Inflexion' section of the introduction

Look at the extract given on the next page and take particular notice of the examples. They tell you all you need to know.

The section headed 'Forming the plurals of nouns' helps you to work out the ways that plurals are spelled, depending on the ends of the words in the singular.

Guide to Spelling Forms

FORMING THE PLURALS OF NOUNS

Plurals are formed by adding -s except in the following cases:

1. When a word ends in -ch, -s, -sh, -x, or -z the plural is formed by adding -es (e.g. *benches, gases, dishes, taxes, buzzes*).

2. When a word ends in -y preceded by a consonant the plural form is -ies (e.g. *parties, bodies, policies*). When a word ends in -y preceded by a vowel the plural is formed by adding -s (e.g. *trays, joys, keys*).

3. When a word ends in -o the more common plural ending is -oes (e.g. *cargoes, potatoes, heroes, goes*). In many less familiar words or when the final -o is preceded by a vowel the plural ending is -os (e.g. *avocados, armadillos, studios, cameos*).

4. When a word ends in -f the plural is formed either by adding -s (e.g. *beliefs, cuffs, whiffs*) or by changing the -f to -v and adding -es (e.g. *thieves, loaves*). Some words may take both forms (e.g. *scarf, hoof, wharf*).

5. When a word ends in -ex or -ix the more formal plural ending is -ices. In more general contexts -es is used (e.g. *appendices, appendixes*; *indices, indexes*).

6. When a word from Latin ends in -is the plural form is -es (e.g. *crises, analyses*).

With compound words (like *court-martial*) it is usually the most important part which is pluralized (e.g. *courts-martial, lord-justices, mothers-in-law*). In certain cases the plural form of a word is the same as the singular (e.g. *deer, sheep, grouse*) and in some words both forms end in -s (e.g. *measles, corps, mews*).

There are two main types of plural which take either singular or plural verbs.

a. words like *media* and *data*. These are in common use as singular nouns although, strictly, this is incorrect.

b. words ending in -ics. Generally, these are treated as plural when the word relates to an individual person or thing (e.g. *his mathematics are poor*; *the hall's acoustics are good*) and as singular when it is regarded more strictly as a science (e.g. *mathematics is an important subject*).

VERB FORMS

Most verbs in English have four different forms. Some have five. The forms are:

the base form, e.g. *talk, expect, grow, think, swim.*
the third person present singular, e.g. *talks, expects, grows, thinks, swims.*
the present participle, e.g. *talking, expecting, growing, thinking, swimming.*
the past tense, e.g. *talked, expected, grew, thought, swam.*
the past participle, e.g. *talked, expected, grown, thought, swum.*

Notice that the past tense and the past participle are identical for many verbs, but for a few, e.g. *grew/grown* and *swam/swum*, they are different. The past tense is used as in *he grew some prize vegetables.* The past participle is used for perfect tenses, as in *He has grown some prize vegetables,* and for the passive voice, as in *Some prize vegetables were grown.* See also the section on verbs in the *Guide to Grammar* on pages xi, xii.

1. *Forming the third person singular of verbs.* The third person singular form of English verbs ends in *-s* (e.g. *expects*), and the rules for forming it are generally the same as for the plural of nouns. An exception is *knife,* where the third person singular is *knifes,* but the plural of the corresponding noun is *knives.*

2. *Forming the present participle.* The present participle is regularly formed by adding *-ing* to the base form (e.g. *walk, walking*; *invent, inventing*). Verbs that end in a consonant plus -e regularly drop the final -e before the addition of *-ing* (e.g. *locate, locating*; *snare, snaring*).

Verbs that end in a single consonant double that consonant before the addition of *-ing* (e.g. *pin, pinning*; *submit, submitting*). Exceptions to this are verbs of more than one syllable with no stress on the last syllable, such as *rivet, gather* (*rivet, riveting*; *gather, gathering*) but this does not apply to verbs ending in -l, such as *label, revel,* which double the l (*label, labelling*; *revel, revelling*).

Irregular forms and other forms that may cause doubt are shown in the dictionary.

3. *Forming the past tense and past participle of verbs.* Verbs that end in a consonant plus -e regularly drop the final -e before the addition of -ed (e.g. *locate, located*; *snare, snared*).
Verbs that end in a consonant plus -y regularly change the -y to an -i before the addition of *-ed* (e.g. *pity, pitied*).
Verbs that end in a single consonant double that consonant before the addition of *-ed* (e.g. *pin, pinned*; *submit, submitted*).
Exceptions to this are verbs with two vowels before the final consonant (e.g. *train, trained*) or verbs of more than one syllable with no stress on the last syllable such as *rivet, gather* (*rivet, riveted*; *gather, gathered*) but this does not apply to verbs ending in -l such as *label, revel* which double the l (*label, labelled*; *revel, revelled*).

Irregular forms and other forms that may cause doubt are shown in the dictionary.

FORMS OF ADJECTIVES

Adjectives can be used in three different forms: the basic word (e.g. *strong*), the comparative (e.g. *stronger*), and the superlative (e.g. *strongest*). The comparative is regularly formed by adding -er to the base word, and the superlative by adding -est.

Adjectives that end in a consonant plus -e regularly drop the -e before -er and -est (e.g. *fine, finer, finest*).
Adjectives ending in -y, such as *pretty,* regularly change the -y to -i before adding -er or -est (*prettier, prettiest*).
Adjectives ending in -ey usually change the -ey to -i (e.g. *dicey, dicier, diciest*).
Short adjectives (of one syllable and with a short vowel sound) that end in a consonant, double the consonant before adding -er or -est (e.g. *fat, fatter, fattest; big, bigger, biggest*).

These and any other spelling changes that occur for comparative or superlative forms are shown in the dictionary.

A different way of expressing the comparative and superlative of an adjective is to use *more* for the comparative and *most* for the superlative before the adjective. This is done with longer adjectives, such as some that have two syllables and all that have three or more syllables (e.g. *faithful, more faithful, most faithful* and *beautiful, more beautiful, most beautiful*).

This form is also used with adjectives like *afraid* or *alone* and with those adjectives that come from past participles (e.g. *tired, refined*). Sometimes the sound of an adjective makes this form more suitable (e.g. *eager, bizarre, correct*).

(from *Collins New Compact English Dictionary*)

Work out the spelling of the plurals of 'fox' and 'church'. Don't try to remember, but use the dictionary's advice. Then do the same for 'dog', 'cat', 'city', 'daisy' and 'day'. Don't forget to use your A4 sheet.

'Fox' ends in *-x* and forms its plural by adding *-es*. So it's 'foxes'.

'Church' ends in soft *-ch*. So that too is *-es*, i.e. 'churches'.

'Dog' and 'cat' both form their plural regularly, by adding '*-s*': 'dogs' and 'cats'.

'City' and 'daisy' both end with a consonant and *-y* (*-ty* and *-sy*). So the plurals are 'cities' and 'daisies'.

'Day' ends with a vowel and *-y* (*-ay*), so the plural is 'days'.

Read the section headed 'Verb forms' and in particular the paragraphs beginning '3 *Forming the past tense and past participle of verbs*'. What is the past tense of 'hurry'? And 'worry'?

Hurried. Worried.

Read the section on 'Forms of adjectives' and write down the comparative and superlative forms of 'fast', 'mad' and 'happy'.

'Faster', 'fastest';

'madder', 'maddest';

'happier', 'happiest'.

This should give you the flavour of the wider help that a dictionary can give. If you are someone who spells badly, and whose mistakes mostly happen when you have to inflect words you can spell, give yourself plenty of little practice questions which require you to use this section.

UNIT 6 USING THE DICTIONARY TO HELP PRONUNCIATION

What this unit is about

By the time you have finished your work on this unit, you should be able to:

- ➜ use the dictionary to help you to pronounce a word;
- ➜ understand the symbols and abbreviations used to help with pronunciation of words given in the dictionary;
- ➜ explain how 'correct' speech is affected by time and country;
- ➜ explain what 'correct' speech means nowadays;
- ➜ describe the limitations of the information that the general dictionary gives on pronunciation.

Introduction

We have already looked at pronunciation in Unit 3. Help with the pronunciation in most general dictionaries takes two forms:

- information given in the introductory pages;
- information given in brackets after the key word (e.g. '**busy** ('bɪzɪ)' or '**nought** (nɔːt)').

Dictionaries use different ways of indicating pronunciation. A common way now is to use the system of the International Phonetic Alphabet (IPA). This unit will follow this system, giving you practice in interpreting the guidance used by the *Collins New Compact English Dictionary*.

Don't worry if your dictionary uses a different system – the practice will still be useful in helping you to unlock your own dictionary as a resource to pronunciation, particularly if it omits to provide any guidance.

Understanding the use of the stress mark (ˈ)

The *Collins New Compact* tells us main stress is indicated by ˈ preceding the relevant syllable; while secondary stress is shown by ˌ.

Thus in any given word we can tell which syllable has the main stress by looking for the ˈ mark; the syllable immediately following that symbol must be emphasised.

Let's take an example: 'itinerant'. This has four syllables. Which syllable is stressed? Look at the entry below and underline the syllable which is stressed. Remember to use your A4 sheet to cover up the answer.

aɪˈtɪnərənt

The second syllable (tin). (Forget, for the moment, the unfamiliar symbols. We'll come back to them in a minute.)

Use your dictionary to decide where the stress should fall in the following words:

- dromedary;
- filial;
- guru;
- doctrine;
- symposium.

In each case:

- include the stress mark;
- underline the syllable that is stressed.

Don't write the word out in IPA, use its normal written form as a basis.

'dro medary

'fi lial

'gu ru

'doc trine

sym 'pos ium

Pronouncing words

Now to tackle the peculiar ways of showing the way words are pronounced. Here is the key the *Collins New Compact* gives to the pronunciation of consonants and vowels.

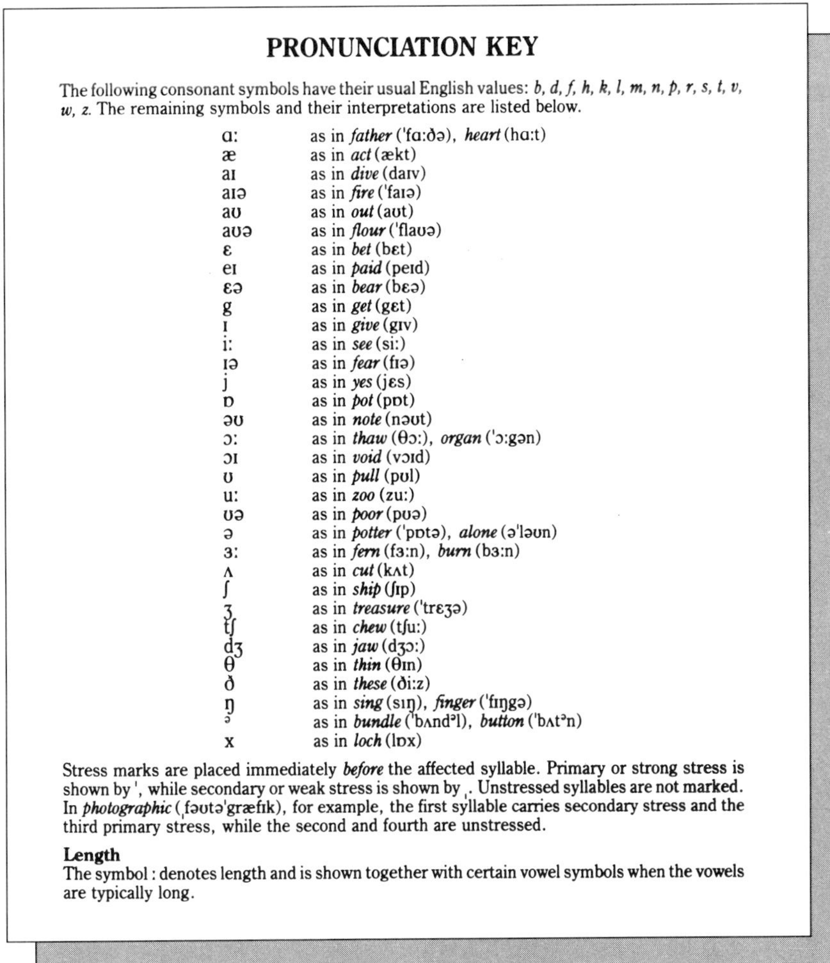

PRONUNCIATION KEY

The following consonant symbols have their usual English values: *b, d, f, h, k, l, m, n, p, r, s, t, v, w, z*. The remaining symbols and their interpretations are listed below.

ɑ:	as in *father* ('fɑ:ðə), *heart* (hɑ:t)
æ	as in *act* (ækt)
aɪ	as in *dive* (daɪv)
aɪə	as in *fire* ('faɪə)
aʊ	as in *out* (aʊt)
aʊə	as in *flour* ('flaʊə)
ɛ	as in *bet* (bɛt)
eɪ	as in *paid* (peɪd)
ɛə	as in *bear* (bɛə)
g	as in *get* (gɛt)
ɪ	as in *give* (gɪv)
i:	as in *see* (si:)
ɪə	as in *fear* (fɪə)
j	as in *yes* (jɛs)
ɒ	as in *pot* (pɒt)
əʊ	as in *note* (nəʊt)
ɔ:	as in *thaw* (θɔ:), *organ* ('ɔ:gən)
ɔɪ	as in *void* (vɔɪd)
ʊ	as in *pull* (pʊl)
u:	as in *zoo* (zu:)
ʊə	as in *poor* (pʊə)
ə	as in *potter* ('pɒtə), *alone* (ə'ləʊn)
ɜ:	as in *fern* (fɜ:n), *burn* (bɜ:n)
ʌ	as in *cut* (kʌt)
ʃ	as in *ship* (ʃɪp)
ʒ	as in *treasure* ('trɛʒə)
tʃ	as in *chew* (tʃu:)
dʒ	as in *jaw* (dʒɔ:)
θ	as in *thin* (θɪn)
ð	as in *these* (ði:z)
ŋ	as in *sing* (sɪŋ), *finger* ('fɪŋgə)
ᵊ	as in *bundle* ('bʌndᵊl), *button* ('bʌtᵊn)
x	as in *loch* (lɒx)

Stress marks are placed immediately *before* the affected syllable. Primary or strong stress is shown by ', while secondary or weak stress is shown by ˌ. Unstressed syllables are not marked. In *photographic* (ˌfəʊtə'græfɪk), for example, the first syllable carries secondary stress and the third primary stress, while the second and fourth are unstressed.

Length
The symbol : denotes length and is shown together with certain vowel symbols when the vowels are typically long.

Using this guide, let's look at how to pronounce 'itinerant', shown as aɪ'tɪnərənt.

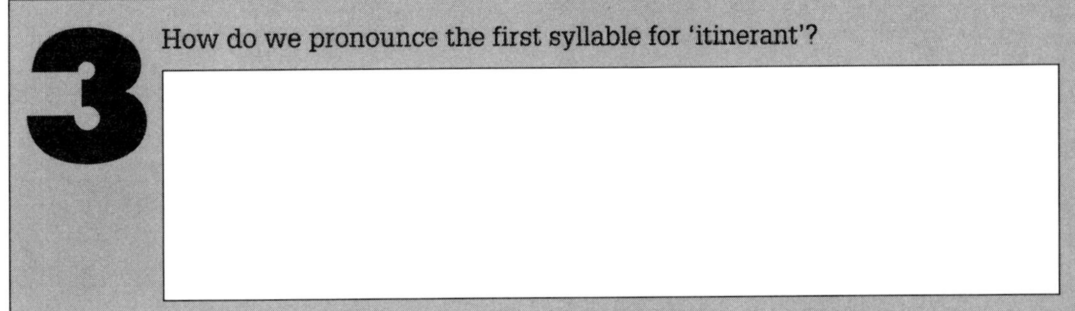

This is given as aɪ and it sounds like 'dive'.

't' and 'n' 'have their usual English values'. The vowel 'ɪ' is sounded as in 'give'. So 'tin' is sounded straightforwardly as 'tin' (in 'tinsel').

We are told that 'r' has its normal English value but it is preceded by another strange symbol, a reversed 'e', i.e. 'ə'.

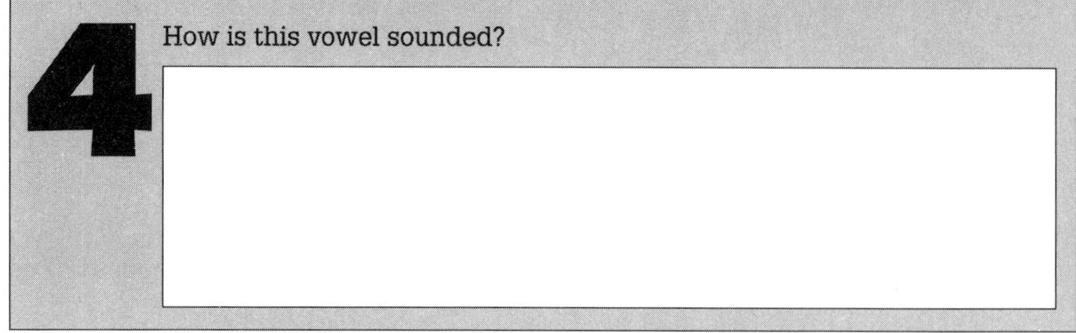

4

How is this vowel sounded?

Like the second syllable of 'pott*er*' and the first syllable of '*a*lone'.

So we are at the final syllable. Here the only difficulty is the reverse 'e' again and we now know that this is sounded like the 'er' in 'potter'. So you should be able to put together the whole word.

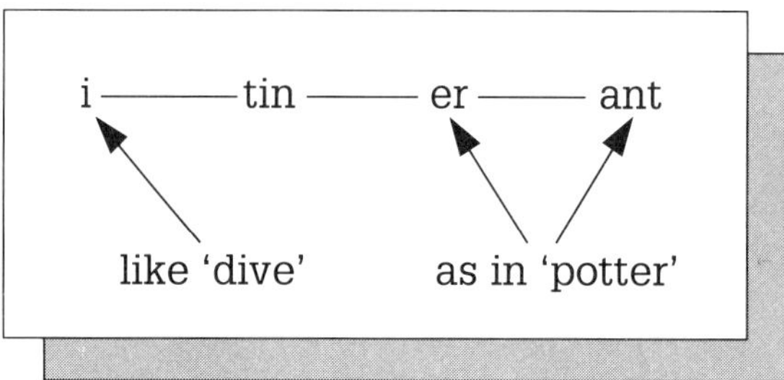

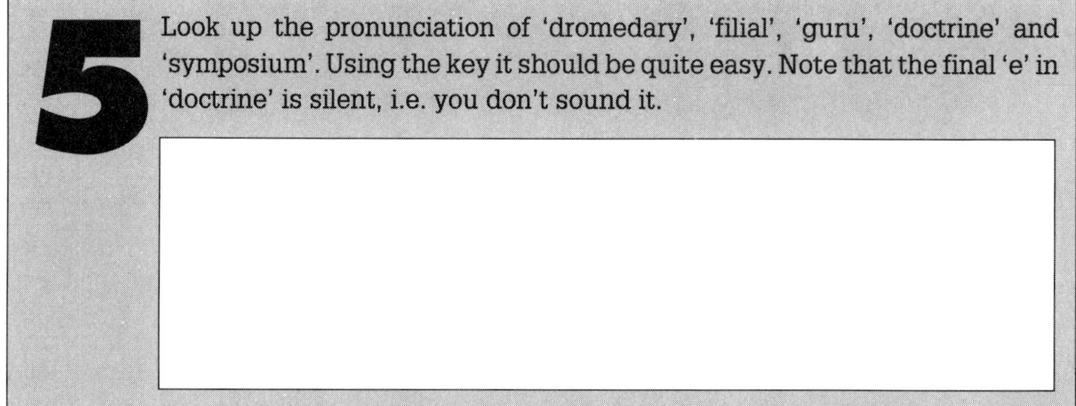

5

Look up the pronunciation of 'dromedary', 'filial', 'guru', 'doctrine' and 'symposium'. Using the key it should be quite easy. Note that the final 'e' in 'doctrine' is silent, i.e. you don't sound it.

Now you can, I hope, use a simple general dictionary to find out how to pronounce words.

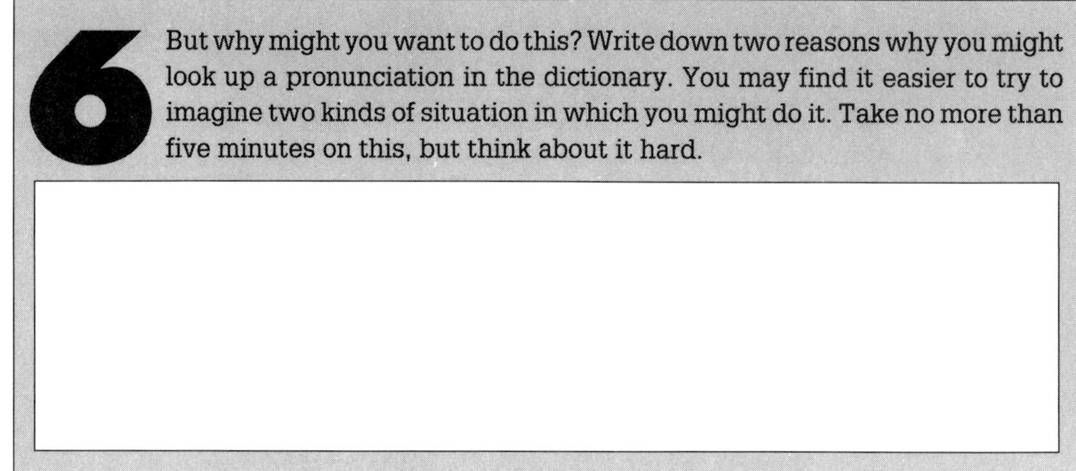

6

But why might you want to do this? Write down two reasons why you might look up a pronunciation in the dictionary. You may find it easier to try to imagine two kinds of situation in which you might do it. Take no more than five minutes on this, but think about it hard.

I have no way of knowing what you wrote, but I had in mind the following reasons or situations:

1 You want to know the 'correct' way to sound a word when this is unknown to you.

2 You know how to say a word, but you want to know the most socially desirable way to say it.

The difference between these two reasons may seem forced and artificial, but there really is a basic difference. For the rest of this unit I shall be dealing with the two reasons in turn.

The idea of 'correct' pronunciation

The idea of correct pronunciation is nothing like as simple as you might think. We need to look at it quite carefully, or you may misunderstand what the dictionary does and does not offer you.

Correct pronunciation and time

William Shakespeare spoke quite oddly, as far as we can tell. He certainly didn't use 'correct' modern English, and neither did his queen. Chaucer was worse. I doubt if you would understand half of what he said.

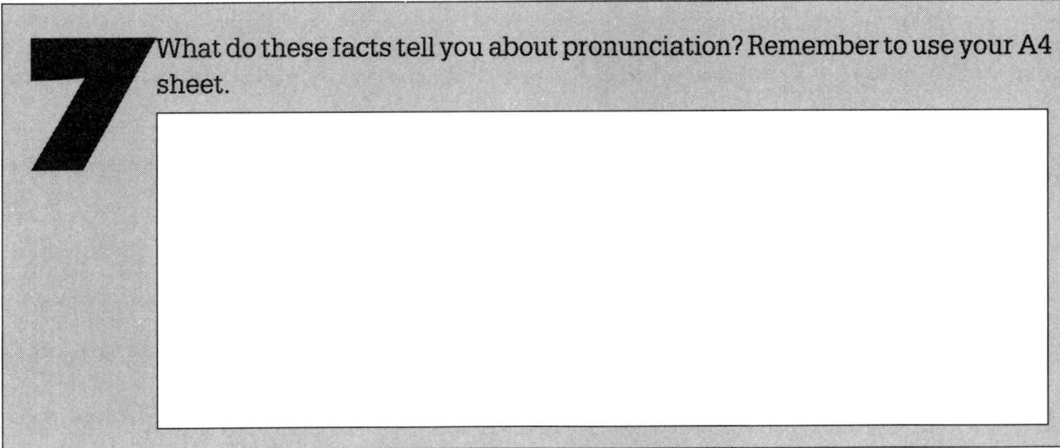

7 What do these facts tell you about pronunciation? Remember to use your A4 sheet.

They tell you that pronunciation changes with time. The idea of a permanent 'correct' form of speech is false. What the dictionary tells you in the 1990s about the pronunciation of words will be wildly wrong in 500 years' time.

The fact that pronunciation changes over time matters in three ways:

1 It helps to explain the silliness of English spelling. Spelling was more or less frozen when printing became really common, but speech went on changing. Thus the 'k' in 'knight' was once sounded.

2 It may matter in using old books. No one tries to speak like Shakespeare when they act his plays, but actors do have to try to make his verse 'scan' and hold rhythm. Often, they have to sound the last part of the word in a way we don't do nowadays. A word like 'served' often has to be said with two syllables, 'ser - ved'. It appears with this pronunciation in a poem in Unit 7. There are many other examples of this sort of thing.

Also, there can be problems with rhyme.

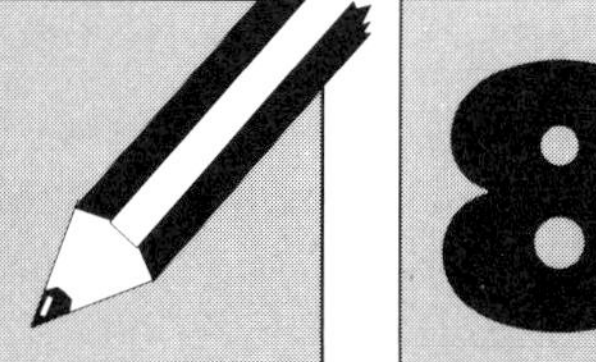

Look at this couplet from the end of John Milton's poem *Lycidas*. Does it tell you anything about Milton's speech?

> At last he rose, and twitched his mantle blue,
> Tomorrow to fresh woods, and pastures new.

The answer is 'perhaps'. Look at the rhyme. Milton rhymes 'new' with 'blue'. It is quite possible that this is a deliberate imperfect rhyme; a half rhyme. I suspect, however, that the rhyme is telling us that Milton said 'new' almost as if it was 'noo'. A transatlantic Milton! I'll return to this point.

3 The third reason why change in pronunciation over time matters is that it is still going on. Whatever any dictionary tells you is an attempt to freeze a language that is altering at this moment.

Look at the pronunciation of 'controversy'.

'kɒntrəˌvɜːsɪ, kən'trɒvəsɪ.

As you see, the *Collins New Compact* suggests that you can stress the first or the second parts; '*con*troversy' or 'con*tro*versy'. It could have listed 'contro*versy*' as well.

There is no single agreed way to say this word. A conflict is going on. 'Con*tro*versy' is probably the natural anglicising of the Latin original, which was two words. This is a common process, moving the stress to the second syllable. On the other hand, the BBC has plumped for '*con*troversy', apparently deciding on one way for all its employees to say a word. Probably, one of these two pronunciations will die out. Perhaps the BBC will win.

Certainly, television and radio are powerful forces for change in pronunciation. Another example is 'dispute'. The English used to stress the second half of the word, but if you listen to your radio or TV set, you will often hear the first half stressed. I hear people doing this more and more in ordinary speech.

The short general dictionary can tell you very little about the changing of pronunciation over a period of time. It has no space for old pronunciation and, like all dictionaries, it is at its least reliable when it tries to catch the latest changes in language. All you can be sure of is that the current pronunciation will not actually be out of date, given relatively recent publication.

Correct pronunciation and foreign English

It would be easy to assume that the dictionary aims to tell you the correct way to speak our language at the moment. But it doesn't.

English is not just the language of the English. Ask any American. There is a very wide range of versions of English, each the national language of a country. They differ in subtle ways – as when Americans 'visit with' someone – and all are pronounced differently. We all realise that Americans don't speak bad English, but American English. The same applies to Australians, or Scots.

Here are some examples of differences between the generally accepted pronunciations of words in England and America. The English say 'missile'. The Americans, however, usually say 'missel'. We say 'shedule', while they say 'skedule'. You know what is coming! They say 'tomayto' and we say 'tomahto'.

I could go on, but I won't. The point is that Americans are speaking a different version of English from ours. They have different 'correct' pronunciations. Indeed, our way of saying 'missile' would be an error, if an American said it in America. If you don't believe me, try telling an American rocket expert that he can't say 'missile' correctly. The reply will be vivid and justified!

As a matter of interest, American is often like seventeenth-century English, for that was when the first settlers left this country. That, probably, is why Milton's rhyme sounded so American. Nowadays, it is usually the Americans who influence *our* speech. '*Dis*pute' is an example of this, becoming more familiar here through television and radio programmes.

The simple general dictionary covers none of this. An American will not find correct American pronunciation in it. Nor will an Australian. This applies to any national version of English which has its own standard way of speaking and regards this as separate from 'English English'. So Scots won't find their correct 'Scottish English' in a short general dictionary; neither will the Irish, nor the Welsh, find their national correct versions.

Correct pronunciation inside England

Even within a country, pronunciation varies as you move around and as you change social groups. There are many variations. No one expects details of these in a general dictionary. Even specialist books only begin to explore the subject!

There is nothing wrong with local accents, or with special accents of any kind such as those which public schools are often claimed to produce. You can't dismiss a Geordie – or an Eton – accent as 'bad speech'. Each is an example of a special way of speaking. But a general dictionary is not the place in which to find information about different accents.

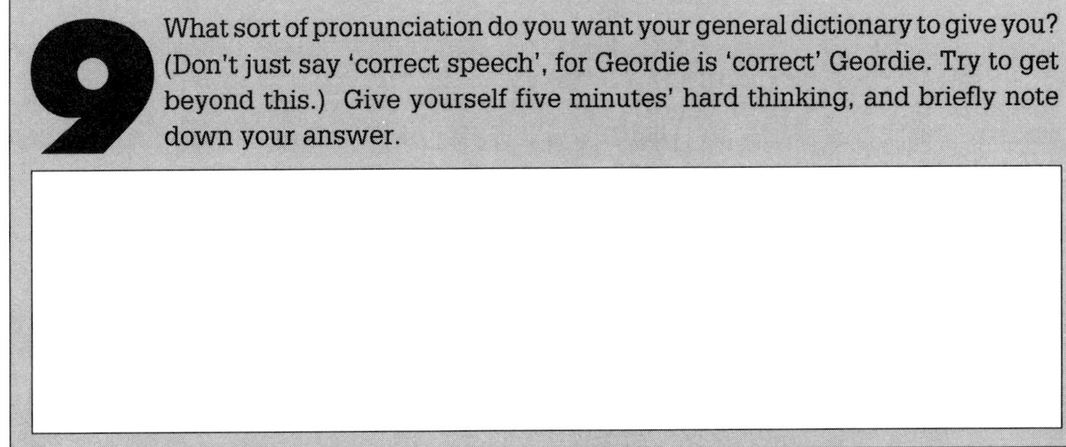

9 What sort of pronunciation do you want your general dictionary to give you? (Don't just say 'correct speech', for Geordie is 'correct' Geordie. Try to get beyond this.) Give yourself five minutes' hard thinking, and briefly note down your answer.

You may have decided that you wanted to be told about 'standard' speech. I think most people will have accepted the idea of a single national way of speaking.

This approach was very popular indeed twenty years ago. The idea was that there should be one correct way of speaking the language, and that all other ways of talking were to be thought of as 'incorrect'. This was *not* a matter of snobbery. The standard was BBC speech, an accent that was considered to belong to no class or region. It was regarded as neutral.

Attitudes have changed now. 'Correct' speech covers different ways of speaking, within certain limits. There is no longer a single 'correct' way to talk. Instead, a range of pronunciations is accepted.

When I say this, I am not talking about problem words like 'controversy', or even 'dispute'. I am thinking of the different ways people speak in Northern and Southern England. (There are similar variations within Wales or Scotland.) Northern and Southern England have alternative ways of saying many words, and both variants are correct.

Take 'grass' for an example. The dictionary says that it is pronounced 'grahs'. In the North, of course, people say the 'a' as in 'at'. Take another example, 'ass'. The 'a' in this can be pronounced, in both North and South, as in 'at'. But some Southerners say 'ahs'. To a Northerner that sounds rather rude!

The point of this is to emphasise that there are Southern and Northern forms of correct English.

Does your dictionary make a statement like the following, in its introductory pages?

> Only the pronunciation standard in Southern England is given.

This – from the *Pocket Oxford Dictionary* – is usually the case. Note that this is *not* to say that the *Pocket Oxford* (or other dictionaries like the *Collins New Compact*) tells you *the correct* form. It tells you *a* correct form, that of the South. For the words it lists it gives 'the pronunciation standard in Southern England'.

The main reason for the decision it takes is, of course, lack of space. Another reason, perhaps, is that the dictionary was prepared in Southern England. Just possibly there is a third reason: an attitude towards accent that has nothing to do with correct speech. That attitude is an important factor in pronunciation. It came up on page 67 as reason 2 for looking up a pronunciation. Check this now to remind yourself. The attitude I have in mind is *accent snobbery*.

Snobbery in pronunciation

Some ways of talking suggest high status, or good education, or just social acceptability. You may feel, say, that a south-eastern accent is more acceptable than others, or that 'public school' speech is desirable. You may feel that falling 'orf' is less painful than falling 'off'.

This is quite separate from correct speech, even in its stricter forms. It is playing social games with pronunciation. At its worst, this way of thinking leads someone to say that the speech of one high-status group is the perfect way to talk, and that the rest of us are stuck with second best unless we imitate it.

But it is very important to realise that the general dictionary isn't taking up this position. The *Pocket Oxford* doesn't say that it lists Southern pronunciation because that is the best or most desirable way of talking.

If the idea of a pecking-order of accents, a scale of desirability, appeals to you, have a look at the following extract from the *Daily Telegraph*, entitled *The (non-U) nine o'clock news*.

Angela Rippon, the BBC newscaster, pronounces some words in a distinctly 'non-U' way, particularly when she ventures among the aristocracy, claims the latest book from Debrett.

Her 'princess' passes muster, with the stress on the second syllable, but she is hopelessly out when she does the same thing with 'duchess' and 'Countess', according to *U and Non-U Revisited*, a new study of upper class speech published today.

Stressing the second syllable – even sounding it – is definitely wrong, declares Rich Buckle, who edited the book. Instead of duCHESS it should be DUCH'ss.

She also falls down on that Eliza Doolittle test of a 'county' accent – Hertfordshire.

Although she pronounces the 'er' correctly – 'ar', as in Derby – she falls into the non-U way of pronouncing the 't' and saying 'shee' instead of 'sh'r'.

This is not all. She is guilty of one of the most non-U mistakes, pronouncing 'Norwich' as 'Norritch' instead of 'Norridge'.

Mr Buckle admitted at the weekend that Miss Rippon was the 'noted newscastress' he had singled out to illustrate his comment that 'Night after night I observe on television our rulers, our idols and our trendsetters getting everything wrong.'

Not everything in her case, he admitted, though.

'I heard her last night pronouncing Rhodesia right – Rhodeesher. Fifty times a week I hear it wrongly pronounced "Rhodeessia".'

But this was a matter on which Miss Rippon was keeping her lips sealed. The BBC said that there was 'no comment' on Mr Buckle's strictures.

UNIT 7 USING THE DICTIONARY TO CHECK THE HISTORY OF A WORD

What this unit is about

This unit takes you to the limits of the short general dictionary, and then beyond those limits.

By the time you have finished your work on Part 1, you should be able to:

- ➜ discover what the short dictionary tells you about the history of words;
- ➜ understand the limitations of what it tells you;
- ➜ understand how words tend to change meanings over a period of time;
- ➜ recognise the difficult job that any dictionary has in trying to be up to date.

Then we introduce you to the problem of older books, where words often don't mean quite what they do now.

By the time you have finished your work on Part 2, you should be able to:

- ➜ see the need for information about old, forgotten meanings of words if we are to read old books properly;
- ➜ see the severe limitations of the general dictionary in providing this information;
- ➜ use a larger dictionary to overcome these limitations;
- ➜ work out the meaning of old writings, by use of a larger dictionary.

Introduction

The larger dictionary we are using in this unit is the *Concise Oxford*. Its eighth edition was published in 1990. You will not need, for the purposes of this unit, to buy the *Concise Oxford*, or any of its competitors. But you may want to visit your bookshop or library to take your studies further.

For even more detail consult the two-volume *Shorter Oxford*. This is available in many libraries. You can also find it 'on offer' in bookclub advertisements.

Part 1: What is 'the history of a word'?

First, it is where it came from. A word may always have been in our language, or it may have been borrowed from abroad. Secondly, it is the history of a word's meanings. Put the two things together and you have a record of its past. The study of the history of words is called 'etymology', and information about it can usually be found at the end of entries in general dictionaries. For example:

dross (drɒs) *n.* **1.** the scum formed on the surfaces of molten metals. **2.** worthless matter; waste. [Old English *drōs* dregs]

To understand this information you may need to refer to two introductory sections of your general dictionary: a list of abbreviations (used in the dictionary) and a section called 'Etymology' or 'Derivations of words'. Here, for example, is the section from the *Collins New Compact.*

Derivations of Words

English words derive from a large number of different languages of origin, and in many cases their development is a complex series of stages reflecting our linguistic and cultural heritage. In this dictionary, for those users who are interested in knowing something of this fascinating subject, the origin (etymology) of every main word is shown, in square brackets, after the definitions.

For words derived from Greek, Latin, the Romance languages, and other modern languages, it is usually possible to give the root word in the form in which it is recorded in the source language. In the case of words of Germanic origin, the Old English form is usually given. If there is no Old English form recorded, only the language itself is mentioned in the etymology, since the ancient Germanic language was not recorded in writing, and so it is not possible to show the exact form of the original. The same applies to words derived from Old Norse, where only the Icelandic forms exist in a recorded literature.

The etymologies, in most cases other than the above, show the language of origin, the root word as it is recorded in that language (unless it is the same in form as the modern English word), and the meaning of the root word if it differs from the meaning of the modern English word.

The source of words

Here is part of the *Collins New Compact*'s entry for 'terrace':

terrace (ˈtɛrəs) *n.* **1.** a row of houses, usually identical and joined together by common dividing walls, or the street onto which they face. **2.** a paved area alongside a building. **3.** a horizontal flat area of ground, often one of a series in a slope. **4.** (*usually pl.*) unroofed tiers around a football pitch on which the spectators stand. ~*vb.* **5.** to make into terraces. [Latin *terra* earth]

1 Explain what this entry tells us about the source of the word. Remember to use your A4 sheet to hide the answer.

We are told that the word 'terrace' comes from the Latin 'terra' which means earth.

Notice how the Latin meaning is from what we mean by 'terrace'. But the entry doesn't explain when the meaning changed, or how.

Already it is clear that this dictionary is going to be fairly adequate on sources of words, but very limited on the history of their meanings. You will see how this can matter later in the unit. But first you need to be sure you can read everything that the dictionary *does* tell you.

Here is some practice.

2 For 'military' the *Collins New Compact* gives the following etymological information: [Latin *mīles* soldier].

What does this tell us?

The word came from the Latin – 'miles' (a soldier).

To get more practice in using your dictionary to check the source of words choose, say, six words and work out what your dictionary tells you about their history. Look also at other dictionaries, such as those in the reference shelves of a library. Refer to the introductions and to the list of abbreviations usually given at the start of the dictionary.

Now you can read the information in square brackets. But what use is it? In most situations, I can only say that much of it is interesting but not vital. Sometimes, it explains odd spellings (try looking up 'pseudo'). And it may well help you to understand why a word means what it does. (Try 'pseudo' again, or 'unique'.)

You may be someone who finds information about the sources of words quite fascinating for its own sake. If so, you are becoming interested in the development of our language, how it relates to other languages, and where they all came from. Many books have been written about the history of language, and libraries will have them or can obtain them. Some are available in paperback. I can particularly recommend Robert Claiborne: *The Life and Times of the English Language: the History of our Marvellous Tongue*, Bloomsbury (1990).

The change of meaning over time

Look up words where the original sources are given, plus meanings for them. Try 'correct', 'linctus' and 'fickle'. What do the meanings of the source words tell you about the history of these words?

The main point is that they show how much meaning changes. In all three cases, and in hundreds of others, the modern word doesn't mean what the old word meant.

Clearly, as I have said before, meanings change with time. They sometimes seem to slip a little over the years.

Take the word 'brainstorming'. I might say to you 'Let's have a brainstorming session.' What do you think 'brainstorming' means here.

You may have suggested something like: 'a process of spontaneously thinking of as many new ideas as possible, and writing them all down'. But my dictionary has the following definitions under 'brainstorm':

1 a sudden and violent attack of insanity;

2 a sudden mental aberration;

3 a sudden idea or inspiration.

None of these describes what we think of as 'brainstorming'. But sense 3 comes closest. The dictionary hasn't caught up yet. This is annoying, but you must watch for this sort of error. It is just the sort of mistake a dictionary tends to make. It is hard for the compilers of dictionaries to be really up to date on all words.

Now let's find words where the dictionary *is* up to date. Look up 'great' and 'fantastic'. They both mean, sometimes, 'very good', 'excellent'. Can you find these meanings in the dictionary?

I can in mine. But written beside the meanings, in each case, is 'Informal'. Another term you might find is 'colloq.'; short for 'colloquial'. This tells you that a meaning is not used in formal, or most written, English. This often means that you are dealing with a new meaning. For written English is usually 'correct', playing safe, while people speak as they like. So changes usually come into the language through speech. A word with a colloquial meaning listed is often a word that is changing *now*. No wonder the dictionary misses a few, especially as the words aren't often written down.

Words tend to become milder and less exact over time. Thus 'naughty' used to mean something a good deal stronger than it does now.

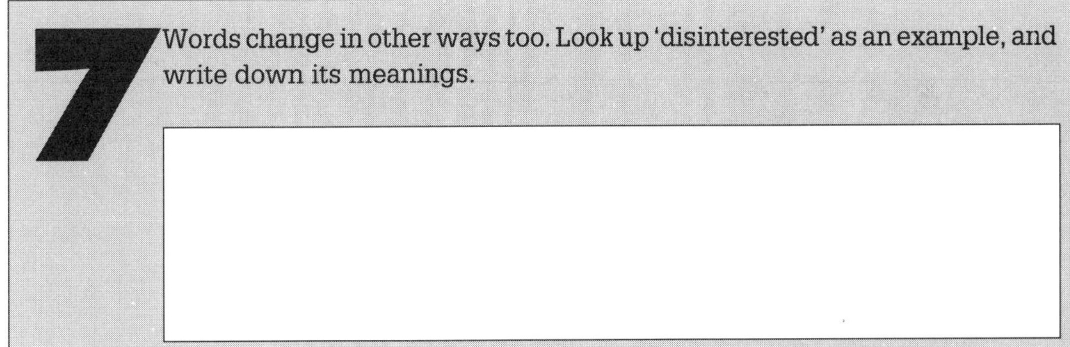

7 Words change in other ways too. Look up 'disinterested' as an example, and write down its meanings.

In my dictionary two meanings are given. Firstly, 'free from bias; objective'. The second meaning is 'feeling of showing a lack of interest; uninterested'. This description is preceded by a comment in italics, '*Not universally accepted*'. This means that the sense, although often used, is regarded by some people as incorrect.

The word is growing a new meaning. Probably, the old meaning is dying at the same time.

So are the 'er' endings that always used to be used when comparing two things. 'Fatter', 'thinner', 'larger'. Now people say things like:

> *Everton were good in defence, but Liverpool were the best side.*

Would you correct this? Perhaps. But do you always notice it now?

I'm not saying that this sort of change is good, or that it is bad. I'm just describing a process. Your dictionary isn't saying it is good or bad either. The dictionary doesn't try to tell you how we *should* use words. It tries to tell you how we *do* use them, and when.

This is much harder to do. So always remember that your dictionary may make mistakes on newer meanings, especially in colloquial speech. Any dictionary is at its weakest here. Luckily, we are all pretty expert at the speech of our own times.

Part 2: Reading old books

We've just been looking at the big problem of all dictionaries, that of keeping up to date with a language that never stops changing. But the way meanings change with time doesn't just raise problems for the dictionary writer. Take a look at this sixteenth-century verse:

> *They flee from me that sometime did me seek.*

This is from a poem by Sir Thomas Wyatt. He is talking about women. Don't worry about the order of the words, which would be different in prose.

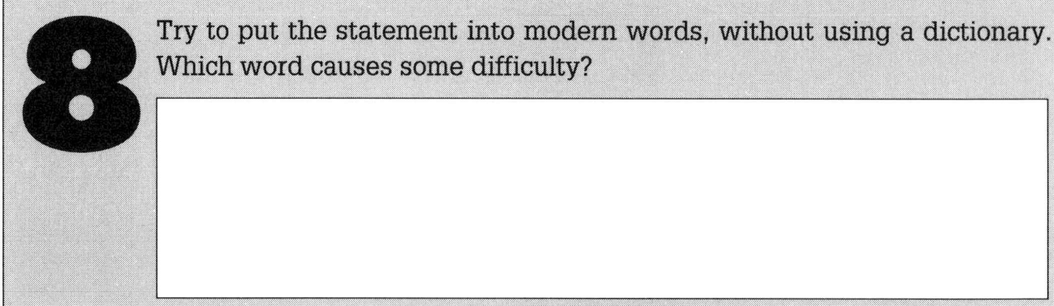

8 Try to put the statement into modern words, without using a dictionary. Which word causes some difficulty?

The word I am thinking of is 'sometime'. We just don't use the word like this any longer.

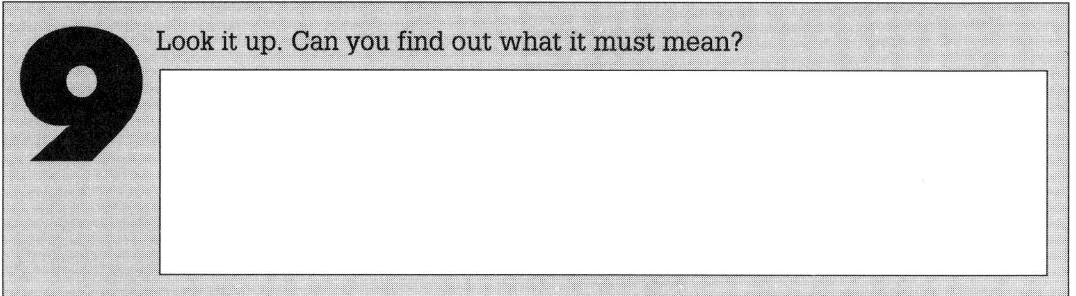

9 Look it up. Can you find out what it must mean?

It must mean 'formerly', or 'some time ago'.

I don't think anyone uses it this way today. 'I drove a motor bike sometime' is not a normal way of saying you used to ride a motor bike. The general dictionary is wrong, listing an obsolete meaning as if it was still in use. But as it happens this helps us here. We couldn't understand the line of poetry otherwise, for the word has changed its meaning.

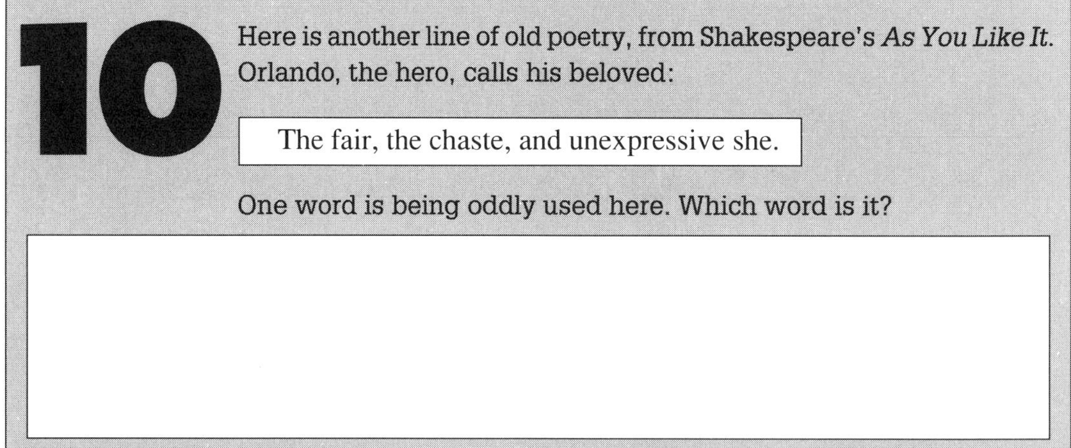

10 Here is another line of old poetry, from Shakespeare's *As You Like It*. Orlando, the hero, calls his beloved:

The fair, the chaste, and unexpressive she.

One word is being oddly used here. Which word is it?

The word is 'unexpressive'.

11 Try to find out from a general dictionary what the word means here. You might have to look under both 'un' and 'express'.

The nearest to a definition that I can work out by using a general dictionary is 'unexpressive', meaning 'not serving to express'. Surely Orlando doesn't mean that his girl is tongue-tied?

The dictionary is no help here because it doesn't tell you about obsolete meanings, meanings that we have left behind. As a matter of interest, Orlando means that his young lady's qualities are inexpressible. She is 'beyond words'.

You can see how changes in the meanings of words can matter. They matter every time you read an old book.

My favourite example of this is 'nice'. You might find a male writer describing his young lady as 'nice' at any time after the thirteenth century. But beware! In the thirteenth century, a 'nice' girl was a stupid one. In the fourteenth century she was wanton. Then, suddenly, in the fifteenth century calling a girl 'nice' meant she was shy. And so on. This makes it very important to know just when an author wrote that his beloved was 'nice'. It must have been a bit tricky paying compliments around 1400.

Here are some more serious examples:

> Then Joseph her husband, being a just man... was minded to put her away privily.
>
> For now abideth faith, hope, charity, these three; but the greatest of these is charity.

These are both hard to understand, for the English is that of the Authorised Version of the Bible, written for King James I. They demonstrate the same point, that sometimes we really have to know the old meanings of words.

What can the simpler dictionary offer us on this?

Let's consider the word 'charity'. You and I know what we usually mean by the word. We mean some sort of a handout, a gift given to the needy out of kindness, not as payment of a debt. Saint Paul, who wrote the original, certainly didn't mean it that way. Look up what your dictionary tells you.

The entry in my *Collins New Compact* has:

> **charity** ('tʃærɪtɪ) *n., pl.* **-ties.** **1.** the giving of help, such as money or food, to those in need. **2.** an organization set up to provide help to those in need. **3.** help given to the needy; alms. **4.** a kindly attitude towards people. **5.** love of one's fellow human beings. [Latin *cāritās* affection]

As you see, the problem of meaning is solved, which isn't surprising, given that Paul's words are often discussed. But the source given in the entry also helped you to work out this meaning. This is always worth a look, where it is given. It isn't a sure guide to meaning, but it may give a useful hint of what a word used to mean.

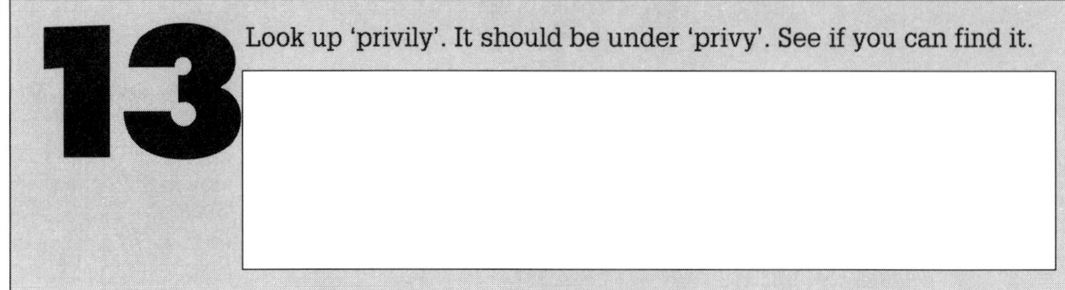

13 Look up 'privily'. It should be under 'privy'. See if you can find it.

It isn't in my dictionary. But the meaning of 'privy' does help. 'Privily' probably means 'secretly'.

14 Look at this extract from a hymn called *Christmas Carol* by Charles Wesley:

> 'Hark, how all the welkin rings!
> "Glory to the King of kings,..."'

Can you find out from your dictionary what 'welkin' means?

My dictionary is no help at all here. Obviously we are getting to the limits of our dictionary. All dictionaries have problems with *new* meanings. But the less comprehensive dictionaries have problems with the old as well. Such dictionaries don't usually give obsolete or poetic meanings.

It is important to know when you have reached the limits of your dictionary. To finish this unit we are going to explore the help that can be offered by more comprehensive dictionaries.

First, let's find out whether the *Concise Oxford* can help us understand 'welkin'. Under 'welkin' we have:

> **welkin** /'welkɪn/ *n. poet.* sky; the upper air. [OE *wolcen* cloud, sky]

This gives us the meaning clearly and it tells us that it is poetic (*poet.*)

Under 'privy' we find '*privi*LY[2] *adv.*'. Under 'ly[2]' we find that 'ly' was used to change adjectives into adverbs. So 'privy' was made into 'privily'. For interest, the *Shorter Oxford* or the *Illustrated Oxford*, with more space, can lay things out much more clearly.

Now let's go back to the line of verse and the word 'unexpressive'.

Here the *Concise Oxford* is of little use and I had to turn to the two-volume *Shorter Oxford* for a clear separate entry:

Unexpressive, *a.* 1600. [UN-[1] 1.] †**1.** Inexpressible, beyond description -1637. **2.** Not expressive; that fails to convey a meaning or feeling 1755.
1.The faire, the chaste, the vnexpressiu shee SHAKS. Hence **Unexpressive-ly** *adv.*,**-ness.**

Thus the meaning clearly fits and the very line from Shakespeare is quoted. The meaning was correct up to 1637.

Finally, the next SAQ should help you apply what you have been doing to a longer piece of writing.

15

Here is the line by Wyatt that I quoted, set in its context. You'll need access to the *Concise Oxford* (or similar dictionary) or even better, the *Shorter Oxford English Dictionary.*

1 Read the poem carefully.

2 Make a list of the words in it that aren't modern, or that you feel aren't being used as they are nowadays.

3 Using the *Concise Oxford, Shorter Oxford* or another similar dictionary, try to work out what each word on your list means in the poem. If you don't get far with a word, leave it. A success rate of 50 per cent is quite good.

This is poetry, so no dictionary can pin down every detail of the words its author uses.

Remembrance, by Sir Thomas Wyatt

They flee from me, that sometime did me seek
With naked foot, stalking in my chamber.
I have seen them gentle, tame and meek,
That now are wild, and do not remember
That sometime they put themselves in danger
To take bread at my hand; and now they range
Busily seeking with a continual change.

Thanked be fortune it hath been otherwise
Twenty times better; but once, in special
In thin array, after a pleasant guise,
When her loose gown from her shoulders did fall,
And she me caught in her arms long and small,
Therewith all sweetly did me kiss
And softly said, 'Dear heart how like you this?'

It was no dream; I lay broad waking:
But all is turned, thorough my gentleness,
Into a strange fashion of forsaking;
And I have leave to go of her goodness,
And she also to use newfangleness.
But since that I so kindly am served,
I would fain to know what she hath deserved.

(continued overleaf)

Since we are dealing with poetry, you may have looked up several words which aren't archaic, but are just used in a slightly unusual way. Perhaps you looked up 'meek', or 'served'. And sometimes I don't really feel we need to look up an old, but clear usage. 'I lay broad waking', for example, is very clear. But I think that all of you will have looked up most of the following: 'sometime' (but we've done that already), 'in special', 'array', 'guise', 'small' (as used here), 'therewith', 'thorough', 'gentleness', and 'newfangleness'. Notice how you can tell that 'small' is an old usage, because you wouldn't choose the word in its modern sense to describe 'long' arms.

Here are my suggestions as to the meaning of the words on my own list.

- 'in special' means 'especially' or 'in particular';
- 'array' means 'dress';
- 'guise' means 'style of dress';
- 'small' means 'slim';
- 'therewith' means 'with that';
- 'thorough' means 'through';
- 'gentleness' means 'nobility' or 'courtesy' (you will find these meanings under 'gentle');
- 'newfangleness' means 'a new fashion of behaviour'.

I found most of these meanings, though not all of them, in the *Concise Oxford*.

I don't know how much success you had in working on your list, but I am sure that the *Concise* will have helped you quite a lot. If you had been using the *Shorter Oxford*, checking would have been easier and you would have found out even more. As so often, a specialist dictionary – in this case an etymological dictionary – would probably tell you all that you wanted to know. I used one to find out about the most obscure old words in the poem, a fact that is worth thinking about. The shorter general dictionary, of course, would have been of very little help.

This is not to criticise the simpler type of dictionary. It is, I hope, to come close to completely understanding it: what it can do, and what it can't.

All that is now left for *you* to do is the Post-test!

Post-test

Check how well you have mastered the contents of this book by answering the following questions, and referring to your dictionary where necessary. If you are uncertain of any answers, or get several wrong, go back to the relevant unit and work through it again.

Unit 2

1 List five sorts of information a good dictionary will give you about a word.

2 Look at *Figure* 3 *Extract* C. What needs does this dictionary seem to be meeting? How can you tell?

Unit 3

1 Write beside each of the following words whether they are nouns, verbs, or adjectives:

a figment;

b livid;

c tootle.

2 Write down what the following abbreviations stand for:

a a.

b adv.

c n.

d unkn.

e colloq.

3 Give one reason why the dictionary is set out as it is.

Unit 4

1 What is a synonym?

2 Find synonyms for each of the following words, by using your dictionary (you may answer in a word or in a phrase):

a deride;

b inveigle;

c suffocate.

3 What is a prefix?

4 What is a suffix?

5 What do the following prefixes mean?

a retro-

b dis-

c tele-

6 Give one example of words formed by each of the prefixes given in question 5.

7 Give two reasons why meanings given in the dictionary can only be guides.

Unit 5

(No questions are given here on the spelling strategy outlined in Unit 5, Part 1 since this is an activity you should be carrying out for yourself.)

1 Explain the procedure you would use for finding the spelling of a long word even if you couldn't spell its first three letters.

2 Are the following spelt correctly:

a behaviourism?

b beutiful?

3 Apart from the entry for a word, where else in the dictionary might you find help with spelling?

Unit 6

1 How does your dictionary suggest that you pronounce the following words?

a reverence;

b terrine.

2 Why is it wrong to say that the dictionary gives us the 'right' way to pronounce a word? (Give *one* reason.)

Unit 7

1 The following is a dictionary entry. What information is given in the square brackets?

OAST n. kiln for drying hops [OE]

2 'The Scots are a naughty people.'

a How could you guess that this sentence was written many years ago?

b What kind of dictionary could probably help you in understanding it?

Post-test: answers

Unit 2

1 It will give you the word's:

- meaning ;
- spelling ;
- grammatical use (what part of speech it is);
- pronunciation;
- origin (or history).

2 It seems likely to be a reference book and kept in a library. It seeks to give a great deal of information and isn't easily portable.

Unit 3

1 a noun;

b adjective;

c verb.

2 a adjective;

b adverb;

c noun;

d unknown;

e colloquial.

3 Because it has to condense a great deal of information and set it out for reference by the reader.

Unit 4

1 It is a word having the same or nearly the same meaning as another.

2 a ridicule;

b entice;

c choke.

(You don't have to have these actual words, but check that the words you have chosen are close in meaning to those given.)

3 Letters at the start of a word to qualify the word's meaning.

4 Letters added at the end of a word to qualify the word's meaning.

(N.B. for 3 and 4 you don't have to have the exact wording given to be right.)

5 a retro- = backwards, back again, in return, behind

b dis- = (any of) –

- reverse of action of state;
- direct contrary (opposite) of the simple word;
- removal of thing or quality.

c tele- = far, at a distance.

6 a retrograde, retroactive (and other words given in the dictionary)

b (any of)
- disarrange
- disadvantage
- disband

(or any of the others given in the dictionary)

c television is the obvious one – but see too the others given in the dictionary.

7 Any two of the following:

- Because a word's meaning always depends upon the context in which it is being used.
- Because the dictionary gives several meanings for some words, and it is up to the reader to choose which is the appropriate one.
- Because the dictionary cannot include every word – e.g. the newly made-up ones cannot be in.
- Because words change through the years.

Unit 5

1 See Unit 5 pp. 57–58.

2 a Yes;

b No. It should be beautiful.

3 In the introductory section or guide to use. Within this, you would probably find a subsection on 'inflexion', or 'derivations of words'.

Unit 6

1 My dictionary uses the International Phonetic Alphabet.

a ˈrɛvərəns (emphasis on 'rev')

b təˈreɪn (emphasis on 'rain')

2 Any of the following:

- How a word is pronounced depends to some extent on context.
- The dictionary gives only Southern English pronunciations.
- Class has a lot to do with the matter, i.e. there is no 'rule' saying a given pronunciation is 'right', but some people like to claim some ways are better than others for social reasons (e.g. to be in the 'in group').

Unit 7

1 They enclose the source of the word; in this case, 'oast' is from an Old English word.

2 a 'Naughty' is not being used as we now use it. We don't call a nation 'naughty'.

b The *Concise Oxford Dictionary*, or a similar larger dictionary. A short general dictionary would almost certainly *not* be useful; it mainly gives information on 'present-day English'.

For your notes

For your notes

For your notes

For your notes

For your notes

Other books in this series

Clear Thinking

John Inglis and Roger Lewis

An invaluable book for anyone who wants to organise and express their thoughts more effectively, or to analyse the arguments of others. Particularly useful for students preparing for assessment, whether verbally or in writing. Topics covered include: propositions and arguments; assertions; abuses of argument; using source material; applying clear thinking to poetry, prose, and art.

How to Succeed in Exams and Assessments

Penny Henderson

An interactive introduction to the key skills needed for assessment in the 1990s. Includes the latest information on assessment requirements for the new competence-based qualifications, as well as vital hints for tackling A level and GCSE exams. The book also shows how to cope with nerves and stress, and helps students develop their own personal strategy for success.

How to Study Effectively

Richard Freeman and John Meed

Enables students to identify their own aims and needs, and to prepare an action plan for effective study. All the essential skills of reading, writing and assessment are fully covered in a practical and reassuring way. Topics include: analysing your learning style; identifying learning techniques; effective reading; note-making; writing; assessment; using additional resources.

How to Write Essays

Roger Lewis

An ideal remedy for the blocks [illegible] students experience when it comes to essay writing. Covers all the stages of successfu[illegible] from rough notes to the final presentation, and includes hints on using the co[illegible] tutors. Invaluable for students at all levels, from GCSE to A level and beyo[illegible]

Acknowledgements

The publishers would like to thank the following for permission to use extracts:

Cambridge University Press: *English Pronouncing Dictionary*, Daniel Jones, Revised by AC Gimson, Cambridge University Press, 1991, on page 18

Oxford University Press: *Concise Oxford Dictionary*, Eighth edition, *Shorter Oxford English Dictionary*, *Pocket Oxford Dictionary*, on pages 14 - 15, 18, 24

The Automobile Association: *Members' Handbook*, on pages 29 - 31

Penguin Books: *The Penguin Dictionary of Architecture*, John Fleming, Hugh Honour, Nicklaus Pevsner, Second edition 1972, © John Fleming, Hugh Honour, Nicklaus Pevsner, 1966,1972, on page 17